1969

This book may be kept

FOURTEEN DAYS

TWENTIETH CENTURY
INTERPRETATIONS

MAYNARD MACK, *Series Editor*
Yale University

NOW AVAILABLE
Collections of Critical Essays
ON

THE ADVENTURES OF HUCKLEBERRY FINN

ALL FOR LOVE

THE FROGS

THE GREAT GATSBY

HAMLET

HENRY V

SAMSON AGONISTES

THE SOUND AND THE FURY

TWELFTH NIGHT

WALDEN

TWENTIETH CENTURY
INTERPRETATIONS
OF
THE ICEMAN COMETH

TWENTIETH CENTURY
INTERPRETATIONS
OF
THE ICEMAN
COMETH

A Collection of Critical Essays

Edited by
JOHN HENRY RALEIGH

Prentice-Hall, Inc. A SPECTRUM BOOK *Englewood Cliffs, N. J.*

Contents

PART TWO—*Interpretations*

TWENTIETH CENTURY
INTERPRETATIONS
OF
THE ICEMAN COMETH

Introduction

by John Henry Raleigh

1. The Life of Eugene O'Neill

Eugene O'Neill was born on October 16, 1888 on the third floor of Barrett House, a hotel on Times Square in New York City. His father, James O'Neill, was a well-known and successful actor, most famous for his role of Edmund Dantes in *The Count of Monte Cristo.* From 1888 to 1895, Eugene O'Neill traveled, under the care of a Scotch nurse, with his parents on theatrical road tours in cities all over the United States. From 1896 to 1900 he attended a Catholic private school, Mount St. Vincent-on-Hudson; in 1900-1902 he was enrolled in the De La Salle Military Institute and from 1902 to 1906 at Betts Academy in Stamford, Connecticut. In the 1880's, James O'Neill had had a summer home built—it was in fact the O'Neill's only "home"— for himself and his family in New London, Connecticut, at that time a rather fashionable summer resort. It was here that the family spent its summers. More importantly, this house provided the physical setting for O'Neill's great autobiographical tragedy, *Long Day's Journey Into Night,* in which he revealed and analyzed the various tragedies of his family: his mother's periodic dope addiction; his father's sense of frustration at having been seduced from becoming a great Shakespearean actor (as he was once on his way to becoming) by the financial lure of the popular *Monte Cristo*; his older brother's (Jamie) destructive and self-destructive traits which were later to lead him to drink himself to death; and his own mysticism, rebelliousness, fascination with death, obsession with human suffering and guilt, and sense of tragedy. Almost from the start O'Neill had, as a friend later remarked,

> . . . six senses. Sight, smell, taste, touch, hearing, and tragedy. The last is by far the most highly developed.[1]

O'Neill's formal schooling, except for one year, 1914 to 1915, at Harvard in the famous play-writing class of Professor George Baker,

[1] Hamilton Basso, "Profiles: The Tragic Sense," *New Yorker* XXIV, Feb. 28, 1948, 34.

ended when he left Princeton in 1907 in the spring of his freshman year, his departure being lamented by neither his teachers nor the college authorities. Between 1907 and 1912 he did a variety of things: worked at odd jobs; went on a gold prospecting trip in Honduras; went to sea as a deck hand several times; traveled with and worked for his father's acting company; married, fathered a child and divorced his wife; and lived for a time in destitution and alcoholism at "Jimmy the Priest's," a waterfront dive in New York (and one of the places which inspired *The Iceman Cometh*) where in 1912 he attempted to commit suicide. Nineteen hundred and twelve, the fictional date of both *The Iceman* and *Long Day's Journey*, was the seminal year of his life. On the 24th of December, his health broken, he entered a TB sanitarium. In May, 1913, he was discharged, an arrested case, but in the interval he had decided to become a playwright.

In the spring of 1914 he composed *Bound East for Cardiff*, a one-act play. His first fame came when this play was produced by the Provincetown Players in the summer of 1916. He captured Broadway in 1920 with his first full-length play, *Beyond the Horizon*, for which he was awarded the Pulitzer Prize. From then on his fame and his finances were assured. There followed in the 1920's and early 1930's a string of successes. To mention only the most well known: *The Emperor Jones, The Hairy Ape, Anna Christie, All God's Chillun Got Wings, Desire Under the Elms, Strange Interlude,* and *Mourning Becomes Electra*. But he punctuated these successes with some rather bad plays, such as *Welded, The Fountain,* and *Marco Millions,* and by the 1930's it began to appear that his initial creative outburst had run its course and that the talent that had created *The Emperor Jones* and *Desire Under the Elms* was drying up. When in 1934 the Theatre Guild, the company with which O'Neill had come to be permanently associated, produced *Days Without End,* probably O'Neill's worst play (although there are other candidates for this dubious distinction), the serious student of American drama might well have felt that the greatest American playwright had reached the end of the road, even though he was to receive the Nobel Prize in 1936. It was true that he had also written, in the middle of his struggle to compose the recalcitrant *Days Without End, Ah, Wilderness!* a charming and successful comedy. But comic plays had never been his aim or concern, although he was a first-rate comic writer, and in his work as a whole, *Ah, Wilderness!* is a sport. *Days Without End* is concerned with the problems of religious belief in the modern world and ends with the protagonist prostrate before a Cross in a Catholic Church. So too it might be said that O'Neill was prostrate, but not before a Cross; rather he seemed to be begging the Muse of the dramatic imagination to revisit him and re-invest him with the primal creative powers. (This wish was later to be granted.) At this point, however, he went into retirement, and another O'Neill play was not to be produced for twelve years (*The Iceman Cometh* in 1946).

O'Neill's personal life was as tumultuous, colorful, and tragedy-ridden as are his plays. He was married three times. Of his three children, two sons and one daughter by his first two marriages, only Oona O'Neill, now Mrs. Charles Chaplin, escaped the ancestral curse that seemed to haunt the O'Neill family and to mark out its members for destruction, self-inflicted or otherwise. Eugene O'Neill Jr., once a promising classical scholar and professor at Yale, ended as a suicide; Shane O'Neill, still living, has led what can only be described as a sad and wasted life; Eugene O'Neill III, son of Shane, died as an infant of "accidental suffocation."

O'Neill's lasting marriage was to Carlotta Monterey, whom he married in 1929. From this marriage ensued his final and characteristic style of life: isolation in a series of often splendid or sumptuous homes (which never became permanent). From 1929-1931 O'Neill lived in the "Chateau de Plessis" in Sainte Antoine du Roches, France; from 1932 to 1936 in "Casa Genotta," i.e., the Castle of Gene and Carlotta, in Sea Island, Georgia; from 1937 to 1943 in "Tao House" near Danville in Contra Costa County, California. Inside these elegant walls two things were going on in addition to the dynamics of the passionate and often difficult marital relationship; O'Neill was turning slowly but surely into a physical wreck and at the same time he was tortuously composing his greatest plays.

He suffered from a rare disease of the nervous system which progressively robbed him of motor control. The initial symptom was a trembling of the hands, a particularly tragic affliction for a writer who was ineluctably wedded to writing in long hand. Thus the late plays were written under great physical stress and anguish—on some days he could not write at all—and at least by 1947 he had to give up writing altogether, except for a few successful and sporadic attempts. By his death in 1953 he was a mind encased in an almost helpless body.

His dramatic ambitions had been immense. After the failure of *Days Without End,* he had decided that he could no longer deal with the present but would have to turn back to the past, and he turned back in two ways: to his own past and to American history. His over-riding ambition was a great cycle of plays, something between nine and eleven, under the general title of *A Tale of Possessors Self-Dispossessed* covering American history from 1775 to the 1930's and detailing the lives of the successive generations of an Irish-American family. He had, in some form or other, written a great deal of this cycle when it became apparent that his disease would prevent his ever finishing the project. Fearful that someone else would attempt to finish these plays after his death, he, aided by his wife, tore up the manuscripts bit by bit. Only *A Touch of the Poet* was allowed to survive. By accident, and against O'Neill's express wishes, *More Stately Mansions,* unfinished, also survived. He had also planned a cycle of one-act plays under the general title *By Way of Obit*; of these only *Hughie* survived.

Between 1937 and 1943, in order to give himself respite from the demands of *A Tale of Possessors,* he intermittently turned back to his own past and wrote *The Iceman Cometh, Long Day's Journey Into Night,* and *A Moon for the Misbegotten* (based on the last days of his talented but disastrous older brother). These plays, fabled by the daughters of memory, are his finest. *Long Day's Journey* and *A Moon* were written in sorrow. In the Preface to *Long Day's Journey,* he speaks of "this play of old sorrow, written in tears and blood" and of the courage that the love of his wife gave him which enabled him to "face my dead at last" and to write the play, "with deep pity and understanding and forgiveness for *all* the four haunted Tyrones [O'Neills]." But *The Iceman Cometh,* despite its somber themes, was written in joy, in the pure pleasure of recapturing a past that he had himself once known but that was not connected with his family. According to his own testimony, the play flowed from his pen. (See the interview with Schriftgriesser below.) For he had found at the last that art for him was a species of autobiography: the remembrance of things past.

*   *   *

O'Neill died at the age of sixty-five in a hotel room in Boston. His last articulate words, uttered with clenched fists, were: "Born in a hotel room—and Goddamn it—died in a hotel room."

2. *The Biographical Genesis and the Literary Genre*

In their mammoth biography *O'Neill* (N.Y. 1960), Barbara and Arthur Gelb have reconstructed the varied autobiographical genesis of *The Iceman Cometh.* When O'Neill returned by ship to New York from Buenos Aires in 1912, he had twenty-five dollars, his seaman's wages, in his pocket. With a couple of shipmates he headed for a waterfront rooming house and saloon on Fulton Street near West Street opposite the West Washington Market. The rent was $3.00 per month, the vermin were omnipresent, and the company "choice":

sailors, whores, stevedores, Wobblies, anarchists, and various other kinds of bottom dogs. This was Jimmy the Priest's, so called because the proprietor, who was really a callous, cynical man, had an ascetic and priestly appearance. At this emporium a nickel would buy a schooner of beer or a shot of bad whiskey. "Gorky's *Night's Lodging,*" said O'Neill, "was an ice cream parlor in comparison." [2] But he also later said that these riffraff were the best friends he ever had. O'Neill's room was unheated, lit by a kerosene light, and opened out through its one window onto a rickety fire escape. There were two beds in the room, so he had a succession of roommates. O'Neill spent no money on food, since roomers at Jimmy the Priest's were entitled to one free plate of soup per day, but subsisted on whiskey and the free soup. His female companions were whores, one of whom, named Maude, professed to be in love with him.

Here he first met some of the characters or prototypes of *The Iceman Cometh.* There was a drunken ex-British Army officer, Major Adams, whose chief diversion was reliving the Boer War and who became Captain Lewis of the play. Jimmy Cameron of *The Iceman* was suggested by one of O'Neill's roommates. This man, a Scot, had been a successful newspaper reporter and had covered the Boer War. Some "appalling" tragedy happened to him and he became an alcoholic. According to O'Neill:

> But always my friend—at least always when he had several jolts of liquor—saw a turn in the road tomorrow. He was going to get himself together and get back to work. Well, he did get a job and got fired. Then he realized that this tomorrow never would come. He solved everything by jumping to his death from the bedroom at Jimmy's.

As with Parritt in the play, the suicide was off the fire escape. Soon after this O'Neill himself made his suicide attempt with Veronal tablets. There are various versions of this story, but it seems apparent that it was not a wholehearted and unequivocal effort, such as usually succeed. About his days at Jimmy the Priest's, O'Neill was later to say:

> I lived with them, got to know them. In some queer way they carried on. I learned at Jimmy-the-Priest's not to sit in judgment on people.[3]

The second location to inspire *The Iceman Cometh* was a ramshackle hotel in Greenwich Village called The Golden Swan, but known to its denizens as the Hell Hole. Here in 1915, O'Neill met more of the characters in *The Iceman Cometh*: Tom Wallace (Harry Hope), the proprietor, who had connections with Tammany Hall, had known Richard Crocker, the Tammany boss, and seldom went

[2] Gelb, *O'Neill,* p. 162.
[3] Gelb, *O'Neill,* p. 171.

outside his saloon; "Happy" (Hickey), a collector for a laundry chain who visited the Hell Hole every Friday and dispensed cheer and free drinks (one Friday he did not turn up, having absconded with the laundry's money); Terry Carlin (Larry Slade), ex-syndicalist-anarchist, Irishman, Nietzschean philosopher, professional drinker, facile and brilliant talker, and a man who had a tremendous impact on O'Neill. The Gelbs suggest that Willie Oban of the play is a self-portrait of O'Neill himself who at this time was an alcoholic, sodden, self-destructive, and full of self-pity. If Terry Carlin had not periodically forced him to eat, he might in fact have drunk himself to death at this time.

Later, on January 22, 1918, after O'Neill's first success as a playwright, at a drinking party in this bar a young man named Louis Holliday, an ex-alcoholic who had temporarily cured himself but had lapsed back into drinking after a disappointment in love, procured a lethal dose of heroin from Terry Carlin and committed suicide. He died before the eyes of the people there. That Holliday had made Carlin, in a sense, his "executioner," and that Carlin had accepted the role, suggests, of course, the Parritt-Slade relationship in the play.

Finally, the Garden Hotel, across the street from the old Madison Square Garden, a bar which James O'Neill, Jamie O'Neill, and Eugene O'Neill all patronized over a number of years, also provided at least one other character for *The Iceman*: Bill Clarke (Ed Mosher), an old circus man. There was also a café in the Village that was headquarters for O'Neill and other intellectuals and writers. Its proprietress was Louis Holliday's sister, Polly, who at this time was the mistress of a Hungarian anarchist named Hippolyte Havel, who became in the play Hugo Kalmar. (See the essay by Doris Alexander.)

Such then were the raw materials out of which O'Neill constructed his play. It hardly needs to be added that most of these characters were not transferred literally or photographically into *The Iceman Cometh* but were altered or transmuted by O'Neill's dramatic imagination.

The references to Gorky, however, underline the fact that *The Iceman Cometh* not only is autobiographical but also falls into a well-recognized literary genre, the drama of "the lower depths." The roots of the human imagination's interest in the conditions of life at the lowest extremities of society probably stretch back into the archaic world itself, wherein it was believed that madmen, lunatics, outcasts were somehow holy or blessed, or possessed a knowledge that normal people did not have. In a more advanced society like ancient Greece, this same belief surfaces in a play like *Oedipus at Colonus,* in which the old blind beggar and outcast, once a great king and the greatest sinner that the mind can conjure up (slayer of his father, husband to his mother), has become, by dint of his sufferings, a holy person. His death is a transfiguration and the place wherein he is transfigured becomes a sacred spot. In more modern times it was the Romantic era, in the late eighteenth and early nineteenth centuries, that enshrined the murderer, the whore, the thief, the beggar, and the outcast as possessors of a kind of outlook or knowledge—what life is like in the depths—denied to commonplace normality. The prostitute with the heart of gold, the great sinner who is first-cousin to the great saint (both of these types are given their greatest expression in Dostoevsky, who had a profound influence on the youthful O'Neill), the idea that normal existence, especially middle-class existence, is one vast hypocritical sham which sweeps under the rug the real issues of human existence (damnation, salvation, the nature of sin, the nature of virtue, the whole problem of what constitutes reality; what is *really* real)—all these themes and concerns have come flooding into Western literature in the past two centuries.

Moreover, this idea, that real life emerges only in the lower depths, is one of the dominant themes of American culture and literature. Thus Whitman:

I take for my love some prostitute—I pick out some lower person for my dearest friend,
He shall be lawless, rude, illiterate—he shall be one condemned by others for deeds done.

Or Emerson: "I embrace the common, I explore and sit at the feet of the familiar, the low." Or Harold Frederic in *The Damnation of Theron Ware,* having Theron Ware describe his experience in the lower depths of New York (not at all unlike the province of *The Iceman*):

I've been drinking for two days and one whole night, on my feet all the while, wandering alone in that big strange New York, going through places where they murdered men for ten cents, mixing myself up with the worst people in low bar-houses and dance houses, and they saw I had money in my pocket, too,—and yet nobody touched me, or offered to lay a finger upon me. Do you know why? They understood that I wanted to get drunk and couldn't. The Indians won't harm an idiot, or lunatic, you know. Well, it was the same with the vilest of the vile. They saw that I was a fool whom God had taken hold of, to break his heart first, and then to craze his brain, and then to fling him on a dunghill to die, like a dog. They believe in God, these people. They're the only ones who do, it seems to me.

In short, the lower down on the social scale, the more clearly and powerfully (so one may think) the elemental and basic issues of human experience emerge. Finally, as one peels away the layers of respectability, humanity itself begins to emerge. O'Neill himself felt an affinity to Gorky and on the occasion of Gorky's death he wrote:

> Gorki is not dead. His genius and his spirit of tragic understanding and pity for humanity which characterized his work will live as long as true literature is read.

3. The Form and the Language of The Iceman Cometh

The Iceman embodies formal elements that are both new departures for O'Neill, considering his career as a whole, and familiar elements. To take the familiar first: O'Neill's archetypal settings from first to last—there were exceptions, of course—were a middle-class home, a farm, a ship, and a bar. It is appropriate then that his last plays should have occurred, respectively, on a farm, with a bar in the background (*A Moon for the Misbegotten*); in a middle-class home by the sea, with a bar in the background (*Long Day's Journey*); in a combined home and bar (*A Touch of the Poet*); and in a bar (*The Iceman*). Further, it could be said that Harry Hope's saloon in *The Iceman* serves much the same function that the ship did in O'Neill's early sea plays. First, the ship was isolated and confined the characters, cutting them off from normal society, intensifying their own interrelationships, and making them in effect a society in themselves, a microcosmic reflection of the great world. So too, appropriately, in *The Iceman Cometh* Larry describes the isolation of the inhabitants of Hope's in sea imagery ("The Bottom of the Sea Rathskeller"):

> Don't you notice the beautiful calm in the atmosphere? That is because it's the last harbor. No one here has to worry about where they're going to next, because there is no farther they can go.

Similarly, the ship crews in the early plays constituted a racial "melting pot," replete with colorful contrasts, including verbal ones, and built-in tensions and interplay. By the same token a seedy bar in New York would have the same racial heterogeneity, and thus the same colorfulness, especially in the language.

Whether on shipboard or at home or in a bar, the primordial O'Neill situation is invariably men, and sometimes women, talking and drinking. In fact if alcohol were removed from his plays, many of the plays themselves would disintegrate. But the point to be made is that O'Neill does not describe the effects of alcohol realistically; rather drink in his plays is a formal device, every bit as much as the Elizabethan soliloquy, used to achieve certain effects. The unreality of the massive drinking that is supposedly going on in *The Iceman* is pointed out by Mary McCarthy. None of the characters, she says (she is describing a stage performance: see below), is visibly drunk;

no one has a hangover (this assertion is not true); with one exception (Oban) no one has the shakes; there are:

> ... none of those rancorous, semi-schizoid silences, no obscurity of thought, no dark innuendoes, no flashes of hatred, there is, in short, none of the terror of drink ... a form of insanity.

What precisely is missing, according to Miss McCarthy, is the final horror of drunkenness, the sense of the destruction of a personality; rather each character in the play is always in perfect possession of his or her own character.

Yet at the same time O'Neill is using with great skill many of the side-effects of alcohol for dramatic effects. It should also be remembered that even scientific opinion today is unsure as to the precise effects of alcohol, and that O'Neill's personal experience in these matters was considerable. Strong drink, first, is the way to oblivion, which is what the sinners and down-and-outers of *The Iceman* most urgently desire. Second, it cancels inhibitions and thus allows speeches of extraordinary candor. Third, alcohol is the great nostalgia-invoker as well, bringing back the past in a special way: roseate, simplified, happier than it really was, falsified, a little island in time that is warmer than the dreary desolation of present reality: the "pipe dream of yesterday." Again, alcohol can be, under certain conditions, exhilarating, not because it is a stimulant—actually it is a depressant—but because it blacks out certain levels of consciousness and can thus give rise to wild and sudden hilarity and to great expectations about the future: "the tomorrow movement." Further, O'Neill was acute enough to see that alcohol is never an absolute, producing always the same effect, but instead engenders a result which is relative to the state of mind or mood of the drinker. Thus when Hickey, the "truth-teller," begins his evangelical campaign to drag the denizens of Harry Hope's kicking and screaming into reality, alcohol becomes for all of them only a depressant: "Bejees, what did you do to the booze, Hickey?" "We can't pass out! You promised us peace!" But when Hickey leaves, "the booze" becomes benign once more.

Last but not least, alcohol puts one to sleep. Thus O'Neill is able to move the various members of his large cast in and out of the dramatic action, without any of the awkwardness or artificialities of repeated exits and entrances, by periodically letting them snooze at their tables.

Another primordial O'Neill formal device is the day-night, or night-day, cycle, with special emphasis on sunrise, sunset, and late or deep night; in short, the long day's journey into night. He had a habit as well of attaching certain meanings or moods to each of these crucial junctures. Dawn usually signifies reality, cold, austere, somber, inescapable. Thus Hickey, the bringer of reality, does not come on in Act I of *The Iceman* until Rocky has turned off the lights and the back room of Harry Hope's is lit by the dim light of dawn. Deep night usually signifies two contrasting things: oblivion and "truth-telling." Act IV of *The Iceman* embodies both: Hickey has told an ultimate truth, as has Larry when he tells Parritt to get out of life, but the rest of the characters sink into an alcoholic never-never land. As for the day itself, O'Neill usually chose, especially in the late plays, a hot and humid one so that his characters will suffer not only psychologically but physiologically as well. Hickey's "reform-movement" is thus peculiarly harsh because it involves sending these sodden alcoholics out into the blinding hot streets of New York at midmorning in midsummer. As Harry Hope says, "Too damned hot for a walk though, if you ask me."

The most important and consequential new formal device that O'Neill adopted in his late plays was the so-called "unities": of time, place, and action. In his first career O'Neill was in the habit, although not always, of employing great time spans and switching from place to place, thus, in effect, constructing narrative dramas: in *All God's Chillun Got Wings* some seventeen years; in *Strange Interlude* some twenty-seven or twenty-eight years and many different places. Whatever the merits of this dramatic method, and there are many, it lacks simply one of the great dramatic virtues, which *Oedipus Rex* classically and forever demonstrates—the concentration or unity of effect, compression, high and continuous emotional pressure—however one wishes to describe it—which the "unities" alone engender: one place, one brief stretch of time, and one continuous action.

In *Oedipus Rex* the crucial action, the killing of the father and the sexual embrace with the mother, has already occurred before the play begins. The "action" of the play then is retrospective, as Oedipus plunges down and back into the past to find the "unclean thing" who is polluting his city and who is, unbeknownst to him, himself. By the same token the crucial actions of *The Iceman,* Hickey's murder of his wife and Parritt's betrayal of his mother, have already occurred before the play opens. Although the audience of *The Iceman,* unlike the knowing audience of *Oedipus,* does not know until the end that Hickey is a murderer, it can soon guess that Parritt betrayed his mother and the parallel to *Oedipus* still holds on a psychological level, for both Hickey and Parritt are seeking to find what their real motivation was. As, at the end of *Oedipus,* the king discovers himself to be the great sinner, so at the end of *The Iceman* both Hickey and Paritt finally find out, or bring themselves at last to admit, the true motive for their actions, which was hatred.

The inner subject or working principle of *The Iceman Cometh* is the vagaries of the human memory—its tendency to rationalize the past, and its consequent inability to know what really happened. While nothing much occurs in the two day time span of the play, the real dynamics are provided by a protean past that keeps welling up and spilling over into the present. Each character must repeatedly make a backward journey, groping back into the past for the self he has lost. In each case the memory spews forth a compound of guilt and nostalgia, self-accusation and glorification—in short, distortion: thus Harry Hope can at times transform his shrew, Bessie, into a loving spouse. The future is really unthinkable in any realistic way, as Hickey forces them all to admit. The present—suspended, isolated, alcoholic—is unreal. Only the past is alive, dynamic, restless, unappeasable. With it, says *The Iceman Cometh*, we can never come to terms, and only death can end this infinite debate of self with self.

Two other aspects of the structure of *The Iceman Cometh* should be noted. The first is that the general movement of the play is from comedy to tragedy. O'Neill himself described it as "a big kind of comedy that doesn't stay funny very long" and thought that Act I was one of the funniest pieces he had ever written. The second aspect is O'Neill's practice of creating rather fully, two characters who never appear on the stage, Parritt's mother and Hickey's wife. Yet so fully drawn are they, the strong and domineering woman and the sweet, self-effacing one (now, of course, dead), that they hover over the play like ghosts as almost palpable embodiments of the spirit of memory that haunts the characters.

O'Neill and language make up a peculiar phenomenon. He is commonly described as a great "writer" who could not "'write'" (see Mary McCarthy). While it is true that O'Neill's verbal gifts were not Shakespearean and while it is true that in many of his plays there are vast stretches of banal and overheated rhetoric, it should be remembered that one of his real distinctions as a playwright was that he brought into the American drama and onto the American stage the various idioms of the American vernacular. Prior to O'Neill, American stage dialogue had tended to be stilted and artificial. Thus it might be said that O'Neill did for the American drama what Mark Twain did for the American novel, or that, like Wordsworth with English poetry, he brought it back to reality: simple people saying simple things in a simple way but giving representation to the most genuine and elemental of human emotions. Moreover, with dialects O'Neill was somewhat of a virtuoso: Swedish, Irish brogue, American Negro, New England rural, among others, all appear under considerable control and with a high degree of authenticity in his plays. He thus used the variety of sub-educated dialects provided by American culture to compose what might be called linguistic "medleys," as he did with his polyglot sailors in the early sea plays. But his largest and most comprehensive linguistic "symphony" is *The Iceman Cometh*: Rocky and Chuck (lower-class New Yorkese); Larry (middle-class American with an Irish flavor); Hugo (Hungarian-American); Willie Oban (middle-class American); Harry (New York-Irish); Joe (Negro-American); Parritt (middle-class American); Lewis (English); Wetjoen (Dutch); Jimmy (middle-class American with a Scottish flavor); McGloin and Mosher (New York-Irish); Margie, Pearl, and Cora (New York lower class); and Hickey (Mid-Western American salesman lingo, with an evangelical flavor). O'Neill is in complete control of all of these accents, especially their resources for humor. Thus in Act I, Rocky's speculations about Chuck and Cora settling down, bucolically, to wedded bliss on a farm:

> What would gettin' married get dem? But de farm stuff is de sappiest part. When bot' of 'em was dragged up in dis ward and ain't never been nearer a farm dan Coney Island! Jees, dey'd tink dey'd gone deef if dey didn't hear de El rattle! Dey'd get D.T.'s if dey ever hoid a cricket choip! I hoid crickets once on my cousin's place in Joisey. I couldn't sleep a wink. Dey give me de heebie-jeebies. [*With deeper disgust*] Jees, can yuh picture a good barkeep like Chuck diggin' spuds? And imagine a whore hustlin' de cows home! For Christ sake! Ain't dat a sweet picture!
>
> MARGIE: [*rebukingly*] Yuh oughtn't to call Cora dat, Rocky. She's a good kid. She may be a tart, but—
>
> ROCKY: [*considerately*] Sure, dat's all I meant, a tart.
>
> PEARL: [*giggling*] But he's right about de damned cows, Margie. Jees, I bet Cora don't know which end of de cow has de horns! I'm goin' to ask her.

Or McGloin to his patron, Harry Hope: "It's not like you to be so hard-hearted, Harry. Sure, it's hot, parching work laughing at your jokes so early in the morning on an empty stomach!"

But the real test of dramatic dialogue is rather simple, on the face of it, and consists in the continuous appropriateness of speech to speaker. As Hugo Von Hofmannstahl pointed out in an early and brilliant analysis of O'Neill's early plays, effective dialogue is not dependent on "lyrical quality or rhetorical power":

> The best dramatic dialogue reveals not only the motives that determine what a character is to do—as well as what he tries to conceal—but suggests his very appearance, his metaphysical being as well as the grosser material figure. How this is done remains one of the unanswerable riddles of artistic creation. This suggestion of the "metaphysical" enables us to determine in an instant, the moment a person enters the room whether he is sympathetic or abhorrent, whether he brings agitation or peace; he affects the atmosphere about us, making it solemn or trivial, as the case may be.

So in *The Iceman* Parritt hardly opens his mouth before the audience knows he is a moral leper, "abhorrent"; and Hickey hardly opens his before the audience knows he is a walking ambiguity and that he brings "agitation," not "peace."

If O'Neill had any one principle, in addition to that of verisimilitude, in composing dialogue, it was a belief in the efficacy of repetition. O'Neill's concept here was musical and he thought of his verbal repetitions ("pipe dream" for example) as the "rhythm" of his plays, the leit-motifs that run through and bind up the whole. Not all his critics (see Eric Bentley below) agree with him on the efficacy of these repetitions. But he has had his defenders as well. The critic Stark Young said that in *Mourning Becomes Electra*, O'Neill "has come to what is so rare in Northern art, an understanding of the depth and subtlety that lie in repetition and variations on the same design." *Immortal Shadows* (N.Y. n.d.) p. 128.

4. The Themes of The Iceman Cometh

The only unequivocal statement about the nature of things in *The Iceman Cometh* is probably Larry's quizzical assertion in Act I:

> I was born condemned to be one of those who has to see all sides of a question. When you're damned like that, the questions multiply for you until in the end it's all question and no answer.

This same philosopher also pronounces the play's comment upon TRUTH:

> To hell with the truth! As the history of the world proves, the truth has no bearing on anything. It is irrelevant and immaterial, as the lawyers say.

At the same time, the play does explore the various enigmas by and within which men live, or try to live.

Philosophically considered, *The Iceman* is a parable analogous to the famous parable of the Cave in Plato's *Republic*. Plato's parable, which is about the nature of reality and man's relationship to it, describes the human condition as analogous to that of a group of prisoners chained to a wall in a cave, which is dimly lit by a fire. By the light of the fire they can see forms, their own and others, reflected on the wall. Thus all they can really see is their own shadows and the shadows of others; they give names to things but they are always misnaming, for they can never see anything but shadowy reflections. Outside of the cave, in the clear and unequivocal light of the sun, lies reality. Plato then describes how painful it would be for the prisoner if he were set free and forced to climb the steep ascent up out of the cave and out into the bright sun, which would dazzle him, and how he would resist the notion that what he had experienced in the cave was not the substance but merely the shadow, not reality but only illusion:

> Will he not fancy that the shadows which he formerly saw are truer than the objects which are now shown to him? [4]

Thus in Act III of *The Iceman* when the merciless but well-intentioned Hickey is forcing Harry Hope out into the bright sunshine of the New York streets, the old man exclaims, after Rocky has said it's a "fine day":

> What is that? Can't hear you. Don't look fine to me. Look's if it'd pour down cats and dogs any minute. My rheumatism—(*He catches himself*) No, must be my eyes. Half blind bijees. Makes things look black.

But here the analogy ends, for while in Plato's parable some men, the philosophers, finally emerge from the cave and stand straight in the sun and see the world for what it is, O'Neill's motley collection of derelicts finally scurry back into the alcoholic darkness of their "cave," Harry Hope's saloon.

One of the ambiguous pleasures of the darkened cave is that in it nothing is ever quite certain or clear-cut, even occupations and names. Thus nomenclature in *The Iceman Cometh* is both highly important and exceedingly problematical. The ambiguity and importance of nomenclature is carried throughout the play by two of its central running jokes: Larry as the old "Foolosopher" (fool and/or philosopher) and the question of whether Pearl and Margie are "tarts" or "whores." Names take on almost magical powers: you are what you are called, although what you are called may not be the truth about you. Furthermore there is a kind of crazy "logic" about names. They are like propositions in a scientific proof arranged in a chain of causation. Thus Pearl to Rocky: "Aw right, Rocky. We're whores, you know what dat makes you, don't you?" Margie: "A lousy little pimp, dat's what." Pearl: "A dirty little Ginny pimp, dat's what!" But when the reconciliation occurs at the end of the play, Rocky becomes once more, "Our little bartender" and "a cute little Ginny at dat!" Similarly Joe Mott is considered morally "'white," though "black" in color, in times of peace, but once Hickey's "cure" starts its dubious work he becomes a "dinge," a "black bastard," or "doity nigger." To Mott is given the single most ironical speech, concerning the problem of identity, in the play:

> Don't you get it in your heads I's pretending to be what I ain't, or dat I ain't proud to be what I is, get me?

[4] *The Republic*, Book VII, Jowett trans.

In the "Cave," then, nobody is quite sure who or what he is, but, unlike Plato, O'Neill suggests that perhaps life is more bearable that way.

So far as the play has an overall statable theme, it is concerned with two sets of distinct but connected antitheses: reality *vs.* illusion and commitment *vs.* noncommitment, with reality-commitment set off against illusion-noncommitment. Through most of the characters the play seems to say that man cannot face either reality or commitment but, through Larry, it suggests that he cannot escape from either of them. The case of Hickey, however, would appear to say that man cannot tell what the reality is and thus where his real commitment lies. Hickey's commitment in the play, the seemingly admirable and sensible and charitable mission of relieving his friends of their pipe dreams, their preoccupations with the past and the future, and all the concomitant guilts, is no less than a disaster for two reasons. First, the world does not work that way; in Larry's words ". . . the great nihilist, Hickey! He's started a movement that'll blow up the world!" Second, illusions about themselves are one of the saving graces of human beings and without this soothing balm people are liable to turn nasty and cynical, as do the characters of *The Iceman*. "No," says Larry to Rocky after refusing Rocky's offer to join him in business, "it doesn't look good, Rocky. I mean, the peace Hickey's brought you. It isn't contented enough, if you have to make everyone else a pimp, too."

The real province of *The Iceman Cometh* is that deep, tortuous, problematical territory of human nature where there are two final questions: how much guilt can a human being stand and how is he or she, no matter how degraded the circumstances, to preserve some shred or semblance or simulacrum of human dignity, however shabby? Though Man has been defined by Nietzsche as the "laughing animal," *The Iceman* would seem to lean to the Freudian proposition, that he is best described as the "guilty animal." Thus the play is, on the one hand, a vast exploration of degrees of guilt, from the easy-going complaisance of the "tarts" to the deep-dyed torment of Hickey and Parritt. But only Hickey and Parritt fall below zero on the moral scale. In them is embodied the grimmest implication of the play, namely that the capacity to bear guilt is not limitless but finite and its heaped-up totality can eventuate in murder. Thus Hickey:

> I even caught myself hating her for making me hate myself so much.
> There's a limit to the guilt that you can feel and the forgiveness and pity you can take.

So too Larry must finally tell Parritt what Parritt wishes to hear—that his guilt is too great and that he must die:

Go, for the love of Christ, you mad tortured bastard, for your own sake!

Betrayal of another human being would seem to be the ultimate destructive act, the sin against the Holy Ghost, and the unforgivable crime.

On the other hand, if the guilt is less than overwhelming, as is the case with most of the characters, then some kind of dignity, however specious, is a psychological necessity. O'Neill's own comment on his derelicts has already been quoted above: "In some queer way they carried on." Their "dignity," their ability to carry on, lies precisely in "the pipe dream" and thus follows their hatred of the man who will rob them of it. The gentlest and the most sensitive of all the characters (and one of the three Hickey wants most to "save," the others being Harry and Larry) is Jimmy Tomorrow. It makes sense then that his reaction to Hickey's plan is the most violent and the most out of character:

> JIMMY: [*in a burst of futile fury*] You Dirty swine! [*He tries to throw the drink in HICKEY'S face* . . .]

What Hickey does not realize is that all the "pipe dreamers" know full well that their own "'dreams" and those of their fellows are a sham but they have tacitly agreed to a conspiracy of "keeping up appearances" and of somehow carrying on. There is a profound psychological "truth" in this insight, even if, admittedly, it is shown in a gross and obvious fashion. Indeed it could be argued that society is held together, even in the highest circles, by some such mechanism of mutual forbearance for harmless delusions. The truth is terrible, says *The Iceman Cometh*: let us gloss it over, although we always know it is there.

But it is wrong perhaps to anatomize the play in this way, for certainly no simple moral emerges from it. Further, many of its concerns and themes are paradoxes: Is it more reprehensible to hide from reality than to face it? Does anybody really know what he or she is actually doing and why? Do we all secretly long for death or is death what we seek everlastingly to avoid? Is there such a thing as truth and if so, who has it or where is it? If we ever did get our heart's desires, would we be happy? How close are love and hate in intimate relationships and how does one tell one from the other? When we feel pity for the weaknesses and failures of others, are we helping them or hurting them? Who is sure of his own identity? What is concluded that we should reach any conclusions about it?

About the only thing that one can say with finality is that life has certain stages, that it is like a dream, and that it finally comes to an end. Thus Hugo: "So ve get drunk, and ve laugh like hell and den ve die, and de pipe dream vanish."

5. *The Reception of* The Iceman Cometh *and the Idea of an American Tragedy*

The Iceman Cometh was written in 1939, its composition coinciding with the outbreak of World War II. O'Neill was horrified by Hitler and had great sympathy for France, and some of the more pessimistic aspects of the play were no doubt inspired by the fact that Western civilization seemed to be on its way to holocaust and general destruction. He felt, too, later on, that the first production of the play should have a relationship to the War. Thus he told the Theatre Guild that *The Iceman Cometh* should not be produced immediately after the conclusion of the War. If the play were to be put on directly after the War was over, its pessimism would run counter to the public optimism consequent to the victory in the War. But he felt that in a year or so disillusionment would set in and that then the play would be properly appreciated. Accordingly, the play was not produced until 1946. (Three reviews, by George Jean Nathan, Rosamond Gilder, and Mary McCarthy are included below.) It was not an unqualified success—many people, for example, complained of its length. O'Neill's critical reputation, already on the decline, was probably not enhanced and may have been damaged further by the play. O'Neill himself confessed late in 1946 that he was "down in the dumps" and was thus grateful when he received a letter praising *The Iceman* from Tennessee Williams.

In 1956 in a small off-Broadway theatre-in-the-round, in a building that had once been a night-club and that could hold less than two hundred people, José Quintero, a then unknown director, staged a production of *The Iceman Cometh*. Whether it was the intimate setting or whether it was the director and the cast or whether it was the passage of time—for whatever reason—the play was an immediate success and went on for 565 performances. (See Brooks Atkinson's review below.) Today *The Iceman* appears to be, along with *Long Day's Journey Into Night,* the most substantial dramatic literature ever composed on this continent, to which the growing critical literature about it would attest.

One of the insistent impulses of American culture has been to attempt to take the old European forms of literature, notably the epic and the drama, and to translate them into the American grain, that is, to use indigenous materials, and to re-create the age-old heroic timbre and the age-old tragic timbre in terms of the American democracy and the idea of the "melting pot." In *Moby Dick* Melville challenged the ancient epic in just these terms; of his motley ship's crew on the "Pequod" he declared:

> If, then, to meanest mariners and renegades and castaways, I shall hereafter ascribe high qualities, though dark; weave round them tragic graces; if even the most mournful, perchance the most abased, among them all, shall at times lift himself to the exalted mounts; if I shall touch that workman's arm with some ethereal light; if I shall spread a rainbow over his disastrous set of sun; then against all mortal critics bear me out in it, thou just Spirit of Equality, . . .

O'Neill, attempting a similar metamorphosis in the realm of tragedy, challenges the historical European notion of tragedy even more insistently. Traditionally, whether in *Oedipus Rex* or *King Lear,* high tragedy involves the fall of a great man. But in *The Iceman Cometh* all the men are little and all the falls have already taken place before the play begins. In short, O'Neill is standing on its head the classic concept of what constitutes "the tragic." For what he seems to be saying is that *all* life, all human experience at all levels of society, is tragic, though relieved at times by humor. This is the human condition, no matter where one looks. One cannot do better than to quote O'Neill himself on what he was driving at in *The Iceman Cometh*:

> There is a feeling around, or I'm mistaken, of fate. Kismet, the negative fate; not in the Greek sense. . . . It's struck me as time goes on, how something funny, even farcical, can suddenly without any apparent reason, break up into something gloomy and tragic. . . . A sort of unfair *non sequitur,* as though events, as though life, were being manipulated just to confuse us. I think I'm aware of comedy more than I ever was before; a big kind of comedy that doesn't stay funny very long. I've made some use of it in *The Iceman.* The first act is hilarious comedy, *I think,* but then some people may not even laugh. At any rate, the comedy breaks up and the tragedy comes on. . . .

And the little men of *The Iceman* are all variations on Everyman.

PART ONE

View Points

Letters from O'Neill to Lawrence Langner

Later on, a mention in the newspapers about a new O'Neill play called *The Iceman Cometh* aroused our curiosity; the situation was explained fully by 'Gene in his letter of July 17, 1940:

> One reason I haven't sent you or Terry a script is that there are only two in existence. I have one and I sent the other to Bennett Cerf to lock in the Random House safe for safekeeping—but not for publication. Don't blame Bennett for not telling you or Terry. I made him promise to keep it dark from everyone, bar none. Frankly, I did not want you to see it yet —in New York. I was afraid you would want to produce it right away and I don't want the strain of any production now. There are other good reasons against it, too. On the other hand, if you or Terry happened out this way, as you thought you might, then I could give you the script to read with the proviso that production was out for the present, and do all my explaining why at the same time. But the idea of trying to do all this in letters simply had me stopped. Hence the secrecy. To tell the truth, like anyone else with any imagination, I have been absolutely sunk by this damned world debacle. The Cycle is on the shelf, and God knows if I can ever take it up again because I cannot foresee any future in this country or anywhere else to which it could spiritually belong.
>
> Well, to hell with that. I'm writing this to explain my past few months secrecy re the completion of *The Iceman Cometh,* and to say if you and Armina, Terry and Oliver, want to read this opus you can get the script from Bennett. I'm writing to release him from his pledge of secrecy as far as you and Terry are concerned. But give it back to Cerf to lock up in the safe afterwards, and *please don't* let anyone else see it. Remember only two scripts exist and it's no time to let too many people, even in the Guild, really know about it yet. And forget about any production.

*   *   *

Terry and I both read the new play, and felt it to be one of 'Gene's major works. 'Gene replied to my comments in a letter dated August 11, 1940:

> Many thanks for your letter regarding *The Iceman Cometh.* I'm damned pleased you liked it so well. Personally, I love it! And I'm sure

From "O'Neill and The Iceman Cometh" in The Magic Curtain, by *Lawrence Langner (New York: E. P. Dutton & Co., 1951), pp. 397-98. Copyright © 1951 by Lawrence Langner. Reprinted by permission of Armina M. Langner.*

my affection is not wholly inspired by nostalgia for the dear dead days
"on the bottom of the sea," either! I have a confident hunch that this play,
as drama, is one of the best things I've ever done. In some ways, perhaps
the best. What I mean is, there are moments in it that suddenly strip
the secret soul of a man stark naked, not in cruelty or moral superiority,
but with an understanding compassion which sees him as a victim of the
ironies of life and of himself. Those moments are for me the depth of
tragedy, with nothing more that can possibly be said.

Letter from O'Neill to Barrett Clark, Sept., 1943

. . . When, in addition, I consider *The Iceman Cometh,* most of
which was written after war started in '39, and *Long Day's Journey
Into Night,* written the following year—(these two plays give me
greater satisfaction than any other two I've ever done)—and a one-
act play, *Hughie,* one of a series of eight I want to do under the general
title, *By Way of Obit,* I feel I've done pretty well in the four war years.
I go into the above details to assure you that, until lately, I have not
been upset by war, sickness, or anything else to the point where I
have quit on my job.

Letter and Interview from "Temporary Retirement" in Eugene O'Neill: The
Man and His Plays, *by Barrett H. Clark (New York: Dover Publications, Inc.,
1947), pp. 147, 151. Copyright 1929, renewal © 1957 by Barrett H. Clark. Reprinted
by permission of the publisher.*

Interview with O'Neill by Barrett Clark, March, 1943

. . . And then he talked about *The Iceman Cometh.* He gave me a
set of proofs, and said he thought I would like the play. "Mere physical
violence—mere bigness, is not important. You'll see that *The Iceman*
is a very simple play: one set; I've certainly observed the Unities all
right, characterization, but no plot in the ordinary sense; I didn't need
plot: the people are enough."

Croswell Bowen on the rehearsals of
The Iceman Cometh

Readings of *The Iceman Cometh* began in May. James Barton was
cast in the role of Harry Hope. O'Neill was impressed with Barton's

Excerpted from the chapter "Past and Present: The Iceman Cometh" *in* Curse
of the Misbegotten, *by Croswell Bowen (New York: McGraw-Hill Book Company,
1959), pp. 309-10. Copyright © 1959 by Croswell Bowen. Reprinted by permission
of the publisher.*

sensitive reading of the part. It was now a new play to O'Neill; it was always this way when he heard one of his plays read for the first time. Throughout the summer of 1946, the Theatre Guild, the cast and the playwright worked on the rehearsals. Everyone knew that in a sense the play would constitute a kind of reopening of the Broadway theatre after the war. It would be like old times—another O'Neill play on Broadway.

There was more pressure exerted on O'Neill than ever before to get him to cut the play. Langner gave him a copy of the play with passages marked where, in the producer's opinion, cuts were very much indicated. In a blue pencil O'Neill wrote boldly the word "no" opposite most of them. When he wrote "yes" it was in a tiny, faltering script. On the cover of the manuscript he handed back to Langner, he wrote: "The hell with your cuts! E.O'N."

In September, as the rehearsals came closer to being finished performances, Paul Crabtree, one of the actors, studied the script and figured out that O'Neill had made the same point eighteen times. He showed the fruits of his research to Langner who, he reckoned, would have the nerve to raise the point—or rather, the eighteen repeated points—with O'Neill. Langner has set down O'Neill's exact reaction: Gene looked at me and replied in a particularly quiet voice, "I intended to be repeated eighteen times!" Langner then observed that *The Iceman Cometh,* like Shaw's *Saint Joan,* would never be properly produced until the copyright had expired. Again O'Neill smiled. "It will have to wait," he said, "for just that."

Often the rehearsals of an O'Neill play would degenerate into a series of running battles between the playwright and the producer, the director, and the actors. Invariably, O'Neill was able to stand his ground against them all.

A typical dispute during the rehearsals of *The Iceman Cometh* concerned the play's length, which seemed inordinate to several members of the company. When all other arguments failed, someone came to O'Neill and told him that the play was running at least twenty minutes too long and that a cut would have to be made. Why? O'Neill asked. It was then patiently explained to the author that the last commuting trains would have left Grand Central Station before the audience even got out of the theatre.

O'Neill indicated succinctly that he was interested only in the play, not in whether the audience caught their trains. It was his play, and it would be done his way.

But as the rehearsals proceeded, the cast's affection and respect for O'Neill mounted. He knew the theatre and he knew his play, and the actors were aware that he was part of America's theatrical heritage. Most of the time, O'Neill sat next to Eddie Dowling, the director.

Dowling, O'Neill felt, tended to encourage the players to overplay their parts. The cast wanted to get the full implications of the play, its shadings and meanings, and O'Neill was always ready to explain his characters for the actors.

"Raw emotion," O'Neill said, "produces the worst in people. Remember, goodness can surmount anything. The people in that saloon were the best friends I've ever known . . . Their weakness was not an evil. It is a weakness found in all men."

O'Neill tried to explain to the cast the meaning behind the extraordinary behavior of the habitués of the saloon—the meaning behind their deeply troubled words.

"Revenge," he said, "is the subconscious motive for the individual's behavior with the rest of society. Revulsion drives a man to tell others of his sins . . . It is the Furies within us that seek to destroy us.

"In all my plays sin is punished and redemption takes place.

"Vice and virtue cannot live side by side. It's the humiliation of a loving kiss that destroys evil."

An eager, aggressive actor asked O'Neill where he stood on "the labor movement." (Two of the characters in the play are disillusioned radicals.)

"I am a philosophical anarchist," O'Neill said, smiling faintly, "which means, 'Go to it, but leave me out of it.' "

Interview with O'Neill by J. S. Wilson

"I'm going on the theory that the United States, instead of being the most successful country in the world, is the greatest failure," O'Neill said, seemingly grateful to have something to talk about. "It's the greatest failure because it was given everything, more than any other country. Through moving as rapidly as it has, it hasn't acquired any real roots. Its main idea is that everlasting game of trying to possess your own soul by the possession of something outside of it, thereby losing your own soul and the thing outside of it, too. America is the prime example of this because it happened so quickly and with such immense resources. This was really said in the Bible much better. We are the greatest example of 'For what shall it profit a man, if he shall gain the whole world, and lose his own soul?' We had so much and could have gone either way."

This attitude of O'Neill's is not confined simply to the United States. It spreads to all humanity.

From PM, Sept. 3, 1946, p. 18. Report by John S. Wilson of PM on an interview with O'Neill at the Theatre Guild Offices, Sept. 2, 1946.

"If the human race is so damned stupid," he said, "that in 2000 years it hasn't had brains enough to appreciate that the secret of happiness is contained in one simple sentence which you'd think any grammar school kid could understand and apply, then it's time we dumped it down the nearest drain and let the ants have a chance. That simple sentence is: 'What shall it profit a man?'

* * *

The ice man in the title, he said, had a twofold meaning. The chief character is a salesman. There is the salesman's old story that when he is stewed he would go sobbing around from table to table in bars, hauling out a picture of his wife and blubbering about "my poor wife." "But she's safe," the salesman would say. "I left her in bed with the ice man."

"That is a superficial meaning of the title," O'Neill said. "It also has a deeper meaning connected with death."

* * *

He was asked which of his plays he liked best.

"That is really two questions," he parried. "It should be which play I like best and which play I *think* is best. I like *The Hairy Ape*. As for which one I think is best—well, *The Ice Man* is just coming on, so—" He spread his hands and smiled. "But really," he added, "I love *The Ice Man*."

Comment by O'Neill reported by Rosamond Gilder, Sept. 5, 1946

. . . Miss Gilder reports, in her radio broadcast, *The American Theatre in Review* (Sept. 5), that at the same interview "a youngster" asked O'Neill, "How can one learn to be a playwright?" O'Neill "looked at his interlocutor for a long moment and then said very quietly: 'Take some wood and canvas and nails and things. Build yourself a theater, a stage, light it, learn about it. When you've done that you will probably know how to write a play—that is to say if you can.' " This, I take it, was not a flippant remark. Is it necessary to add that the experienced playwright was here advising a beginner to remember that what he has to show and say must be conveyed in terms of physical theater?

From Eugene O'Neill: The Man and His Plays, *by Barrett Clark (New York: Dover Publications, Inc., 1947), p. 153. Copyright © 1926 by Barrett Clark. Reprinted by permission of the publisher.*

Interview with O'Neill by S. J. Woolf

. . . When I asked him how long a play should be he said: "As long as necessary to tell the story. No play is too long that holds the interest of its audience. If a short play is tiresome it is too long and if a long play is absorbing until the fall of the last curtain no one will pull out his watch to look at the time."

*   *   *

Most of O'Neill's talk, while I was sketching, was of the theatre, and much of it was reminiscent. Several times he mentioned his father, the celebrated James O'Neill. As a child, the playwright traveled widely with the elder O'Neill's troupe. "Almost the first words of my father I remember," he said, "are, 'The theatre is dying.' And those words seem to me as true today as when he said them. But the theatre must be a hardy wench, for although she is still ailing, she will never die as long as she offers an escape."

*   *   *

It was no surprise that a dramatist who has consistently written "experimental" plays should talk at length about theatre technique. New techniques, O'Neill pointed out, often amount to no more than fads. He mentioned expressionism as one fad that had waxed and waned in the modern theatre, and while he poked fun at that movement's excesses, he was quick to add that it had had "some good influence in playwriting. The trouble with a fad—and this holds true for any form of art—is that it affords an opportunity for people who do not know the technique to pose as artists. There are as well-established rules for the theatre as there are for painting and music. The only ones who can successfully break the rules are the people who know them. A knowledge of rules is necessary, even if adhering to tradition is not."

*   *   *

He sat still for some minutes, saying nothing and staring out into space. In one of his thin hands was the ever-present cigarette—a mild brand with a cork tip and cotton filter. His thoughts seemed far away and I hesitated to break the silence. Suddenly he looked up and a

"Interview with O'Neill by S. J. Woolf" from **The New York Times Magazine** (*September 15, 1946*), *pp. 11, 61, 62. Copyright © 1946 by The New York Times Company. Reprinted by permission of the publisher and Muriel Woolf Hobson.*

smile spread over his face. He said that he had been thinking of the past.

He added: "I am not saying that some of the actors and actresses who interpreted my plays did not add something to them. But, after all, even an owl thinks her owlets are the most beautiful babies in the world and that's the way an author feels about his stage children. It is for this reason that I always attend the rehearsals of my plays. While I do not want to change the personalities of the artists acting in them, I want to make it clear to them what was in my mind when I wrote the play.

"I confess, though, that I have never been completely satisfied with anything that I have done and I constantly rewrite my plays until they are produced and even then I always see things which I could improve and I regret that it is too late to make more changes.

"For, after all, anyone who creates anything must feel deeply. Like Shaw, he may cover up his sincerity with humor, he may make light of his efforts, but those efforts are nevertheless heart-breaking."

Interview with O'Neill by Karl Schriftgriesser

"I knew 'em all," he said. "I've known 'em all for years." His voice dropped gropingly into his remembrance of things past. "All these people I have written about, I once knew." Another long pause. "I do not think that you can write anything of value or understanding about the present. You can only write about life if it is far enough in the past. The present is too much mixed up with superficial values; you can't know which thing is important and which is not.

"The past which I have chosen is one I knew. The man who owns this saloon, Harry Hope, and all the others—the Anarchists and Wobblies and French Syndicalists, the broken men, the tarts, the bartenders and even the saloon itself—are real. It's not just one place, perhaps, but it is several places that I lived in at one time or another"—he let his brooding eyes wander over the present living room, with its books and comfortable furniture, and his beloved collection of records neatly stacked on shelves—"places I once knew put together in one.

"What have I done with this setting? Well, I've tried to show the inmates of Harry Hope's saloon there with their dreams. Some, you see, have just enough money from home to keep them going; but most of 'em keep from starving with the aid of the free lunch. This

"*Interview with O'Neill by Karl Schriftgriesser*" from The New York Times, Sunday Drama Section (*October 6, 1946*) *pp. 1, 3. Copyright © 1946 by The New York Times Company. Reprinted by permission of the publisher.*

old Tammany politician who runs the place lives with his dreams, too, and he loves these people for he is one of them in his way.

"You ask, what is the significance, what do these people mean to us today? Well, all I can say is that it is a play about pipe dreams. And the philosophy is that there is always one dream left, one final dream, no matter how low you have fallen, down there at the bottom of the bottle. I know, because I saw it."

*   *   *

. . . Its philosophy is eternal and universal, O'Neill thinks: "It will take man," he says, "a million years to grow up and obtain a soul."

O'Neill talked, too, about the title. To him titles are a matter of great importance.

"I always try to get into the title the surface meaning and at the same time the deeper significance."

The surface meaning of "The Iceman Cometh" stems from a sardonic wisecrack, often repeated by one of the characters, who tells people he has left his wife safe at home with the iceman. The play revolves around this. But as it proceeds the "iceman," who started as a ribald joke, takes on a different, deeper and even terrifying meaning and before the end becomes Death itself.

The idea for "Iceman" came to him suddenly. Because he knew all the characters so well there "was not so much hard work as if I had had to dig them out." Once started, the work "flowed right along, page after page," he recalled, his deep eyes happy with the memory. Later he revised it once.

"The Iceman Cometh" apparently was created more easily than others of his plays. "I don't just write plays," he explained. "I make many notes over a long period. Then I write a scenario of 20,000 or so words. I draw out all the scenes from my own strange conception of perspective, which I understand, even if directors don't always."

Review of the 1946 production of *The Iceman Cometh* by George Jean Nathan

With the appearance of *The Iceman Cometh,* our theatre has become dramatically alive again. It makes most of the plays of other American playwrights produced during the more than twelve-year period of O'Neill's absence look comparatively like so much damp

"Review of the 1946 production of The Iceman Cometh," *by George Jean Nathan. From* The Theatre Book of the Year, *1946-1947 (New York: Alfred A. Knopf, Inc., 1947), pp. 93-96, 110-11. Copyright © 1947 by George Jean Nathan. Reprinted by permission of Mrs. Julie Haydon Nathan.*

tissue paper. In it there is an understanding of the deeper elements of human nature, a comprehension of the confused instincts that make up the life of mortals, and an evocation of pity for the tortured existence of dazed mankind that not merely most but all of those plays in combination have not faintly suggested. It is, in short, one of the best of its author's works and one that again firmly secures his position not only as the first of American dramatists but, with Shaw and O'Casey, one of the three really distinguished among the world's living.

These, I appreciate, are big words and probably contributive to the suspicion that their inditer has forgone his old Phyrronism. They are also doubtless obnoxious and challenging to such persons as either resent what seems to be extravagant praise at the expense of other playwrights or are constitutionally averse to superlatives of any kind and ready to throw off their coats if anyone has the gall to say even that Bach was the greatest composer who ever lived or that horseradish sauce is the best of all things to go with boiled beef. But the words, I believe, are none the less in good order. If they are not and if the play is not what I think it is, I am prepared to atone for my ignorance by presenting gratis to anyone who can offer convincing contrary evidence the complete bound works of all our American playwrights from Bronson Howard through Charles Klein, David Belasco and Augustus Thomas down to the geniuses responsible for *Joan of Lorraine, Another Part of the Forest, Dream Girl,* and *Maid in the Ozarks.*

Laying hold of an assortment of social outcasts quartered in a disreputable saloon on the fringe of New York in the year 1912 and introducing into their drunken semblance of contentful hope an allergy in the shape of a Werlean traveling salesman, O'Neill distils from them, slowly but inexorably, the tragedy that is death in life. Superficially at times suggesting a cross between Gorki's *The Lower Depths* and Saroyan's *The Time of Your Life,* let alone Ibsen's *The Wild Duck,* the play with its author's uncommon dramaturgical skill gradually weaves its various vagrant threads into a solid thematic pattern and in the end achieves a purge and mood of compassion that mark it apart from the bulk of contemporary drama. There are repetitions in the middle sections which O'Neill has deemed necessary to the impact of the play but which in this opinion might be got rid of with no loss. There is also still an excess of profanity, for all the author's liberal cutting, that becomes disturbing to any ear that gags at such overemphasis. And since the uncut version of *Hamlet,* which is a good play too, can be played in its entirety in little more than three and a half hours, the longer running time of *The Iceman Cometh* may seem to some, and quite rightly, not only superfluous but a little pretentious. Yet small matter. In the whole history of drama there has been only one really perfect tragedy—incidentally, only one-third as long—and, while this of O'Neill's is scarcely to be compared with it, it still rises far above its possible errors.

With a few nimble strokes, O'Neill pictures vividly the innards of even the least of his variegated characters, from the one-time circus grifter to the one-time police lieutenant, from the quondam boss of a Negro gambling den to the erstwhile Boer War correspondent, and from the night and day bartenders and the wreck of a college graduate to the former editor of Anarchist magazines and the old captain once in the British armed services. Only in the characters of his three street-walkers does he work rather obviously; truthfully, perhaps, but in a theatrically routine manner. Yet in his major figures, Slade, the one-time Syndicalist-Anarchist, Hickey, the hardware salesman, Hope, the proprietor of the saloon, etc., the hand is as steady and sure as ever.

The long monologue, only now and then momentarily interrupted, wherein toward the drama's conclusion the salesman relates the relief from himself secured by the murder of his wife, is one of the most impressive pieces of writing in contemporary dramatic literature: emotionally searching and definitely moving. The relations of Slade and the young man with memory of his betrayed mother on his agonized conscience are maneuvered with high suspensive dexterity, even if at one or two points to the hypercritical slightly overplanted. The dialogue throughout is driving; there is robust humor to alleviate the atmospheric sordidness; and out of the whole emerges in no small degree the profound essences of authentic tragedy.

In the author's own analysis of his play as he has confided it to me the dominant intention has been a study in the workings of strange friendship. That intention, it is not to be gainsaid, has been fully realized. But as I read the script and see it in stage action it seems to me that, far above and beyond it, there rises the theme of the tragedy which lies in bogus self-substantiation and the transient, pitiable satisfaction which it bequeaths. That, however, is the play's virtue: to different men it may convey different things. But to all with any emotional understanding and to all with any appreciation of the drama it must convey the satisfaction of a theatre that, if only for a short while, has again come into its rightful own.

*   *   *

He is a stickler for casting and direction. As to the latter, his constant concern is any sentimentalization of his work. "Where sentiment exists," he says, "there is sufficient of it in the characters, and any directional emphasis would throw it out of all proportion and make it objectionable." As to casting, he is generally opposed to so-called name actors. "They distract attention from the play to themselves," he argues. "My plays are not for stars but for simply good actors. Besides,

you can never count on the idiosyncrasies of stars; they may not stick
to a play and may so damage its chances on the road. I'm afraid of
them, as I've had some experience with them. Also, they sometimes
want you to change certain things in your play. Not for me!"

To return, finally, to *The Iceman Cometh,* I have already twice
remarked that it may very roughly be described as a kind of American
The Lower Depths. Like that play of Gorki's, though it in few other
ways resembles it, it treats of a group of degenerate outcasts and the
advent among them of a man with a philosophy of life new and disturbing to them. Its language is realistic, at times over-violently so;
its cast of alcoholic down-and-outs includes gamblers, grafting cops,
circus lot sharpers, whores, pimps, Anarchist riff-raff, military failures,
college-educated wastrels, stool-pigeons, *et al.;* and it is written in four
parts. It attests again to the fact, lost upon some of O'Neill's critics,
that he is far from lacking a healthy sense of humor. Some of the comedy writing is irresistible. It also demonstrates again the most barbed
appreciation of character known to any of his American playwriting
contemporaries. And it embraces, among many other things, the most
pitifully affecting picture of a woman—the unseen wife of the protagonist—that I, for one, have encountered in many years of playgoing.

Among the criticisms of the play is the argument that the characters
"do not grow." That they do not grow is O'Neill's specific dramatic
theme. Human beings sometimes change but change is not necessarily
growth. Change is frequently impermanent and retrogressive rather
than advancing as O'Neill indicates. Another argument is that Hickey,
the salesman of Death, in the end "explains himself with a textbook
clarity that robs him of a truly dramatic role in the play, or a really
human complexity." What of Nina in *The Sea Gull?* And a third con-
descendingly observes, "As for O'Neill's 'thesis,' it would seem to be
that men cannot live without illusions; hardly a new or very disputable idea." Hardly new, granted; but not very disputable? Come, come.
What of the sufficient disputations on occasion of Ibsen, Strindberg,
Zola, Hauptmann, Tolstoi, Wedekind, Shaw . . . ?

Rosamond Gilder: *"The Iceman Cometh"*

Like Peer Gynt's onion, the story of *The Iceman* has its layers and
layers of meaning. It touches on a dozen different themes and relationships. While the subsidiary characters are separate microcosms of

From "The Iceman Cometh," *by Rosamond Gilder, in* Theatre Arts Anthology
*(New York: Theatre Arts Books, 1950), pp. 664-65. Copyright 1946 by Theatre Arts,
Inc. Copyright 1950 by Theatre Arts Books. Reprinted by permission of Theatre
Arts Books, N.Y.*

despair, the three chief figures, Hickey, Larry, and Parritt, are three aspects of man—each element loving and loathing the other. The play is in a very special sense a summary of much of O'Neill's past writing. Superficially it goes back as far as the vigorous sea plays with which he made his debut. Its frank barroom talk, its conventional tarts, its amiable drunks, its passion and violence are reminders of the impact of his first writing. Don Parritt, the boy rejected by his mother, haunted by the guilt of his betrayal of her, which is nothing less than matricide, recalls O'Neill's days of absorption in psychoanalysis while Larry the philosopher is the O'Neill who attempted a detachment and objectivity never native to him.

But it is through Hickey who has known the love that passeth understanding and has rejected it that we glimpse O'Neill's ultimate meaning. Blind, besotted, and misguided, man haunted by death lives by lies. "The lie of a pipe dream is what gives life to the whole misbegotten mad lot of us, drunk or sober," Larry says at the opening of the play. But there is a truth which is not the truth of alcohol or political shibboleths, or psychology or philosophy, or even the truth of "facing the truth" which Hickey preaches. The greatest illusion of all is to believe that disillusionment—the unaided processes of the intellect—can solve man's dilemma. There is a force that, like the love that Hickey's wife bore him, is made of understanding and forgiveness. Man finds such love intolerable. "I couldn't forgive her for forgiving me," Hickey explains. "I caught myself hating her for making me hate myself so much. There is a limit to the guilt you can feel and the forgiveness and pity you can take." And so man denies, destroys and blasphemes such love, only in the end to find that this too will be forgiven. The denizens of Hickey's world and of the world at large find a simple answer to Hickey's final revelation. The man is mad! Hamlet to the contrary notwithstanding, there is nothing more in heaven and earth than can be compassed in any current philosophy. Pass the bottle. Drink up. What the hell! It's a good play, brother, why bother?

And it is a good play, excellently acted and directed, full of substance. It would seem that it could readily be compressed into a more reasonable running time, but O'Neill has a tendency to shirk the task of selection and condensation. He has so much to say that even this four-and-a-half-hour play must seem short to a man who thinks in terms of trilogies and nine-play cycles. For the onlooker, however, a shorter play would have brought into sharper focus the conflicting and merging elements of the three chief figures of the fable. The subsidiary characters are not sufficiently important or rounded to demand the time and attention they absorb. They are each set in their groove in the first half hour. They never emerge from the pattern to take on human proportions. The reiterated pattern of their false redemption and its death-dealing effect becomes tedious. Mr. O'Neill seems to underestimate the ability of the audience to grasp his idea, or perhaps more truly he has so fond a remembrance softened by time and distance of these denizens of his kingdom of despair that he cannot bear to tear up the sketches he has made in his mind's eye as he sat with them at marble-topped tables or leaned against mahogany bars in a hundred saloons the world over.

But the length of *The Iceman,* though it adds very little to the characterizations so boldly sketched in the first scenes, does permit an interesting orchestration of effects which Mr. Dowling has developed in this direction. The stage is almost continuously peopled by all the characters in the play at once. There is little movement; there is only an antiphonal development of themes. Besides the pipe-dream motive, which is developed in turn by each of the characters playing in groups of threes and fours, there is also the predominant, haunting theme of Death. O'Neill's bums are all in pursuit of forgetfulness, of sleep, of death. They spend most of their time in blissful or tormented alcoholic slumber. O'Neill uses this device to bring them in and out of the action without making them leave the stage. As the play progresses, the way the tables are grouped in the backroom and bar and the manner in which actors are grouped around them—slumped over asleep or sitting in a deathly daydream—provides a constant visual comment on the developing theme.

José Quintero: "Postscript to a Journey"

On March 15, 1956, I went to see Carlotta Monterey O'Neill for the first time, to discuss a possible revival of her late husband's tragedy *The Iceman Cometh.*

The Circle in the Square Theatre, of which I am director and one of the producers, had been yearning to do a work by Eugene O'Neill for a long time. But whenever we made inquiries we always met the same answer, "All the works of Mr. O'Neill, are, at the moment, not available for production." Mrs. O'Neill's invitation to call seemed promising, and I was a hopeful, if anxious, visitor. I was frightened and nervous, for my hostess was, after all, the widow of America's greatest dramatist. It was a remarkable and, as it turned out, a portentous meeting. I saw a lady of medium height, her black hair pulled back and cut short at the back of the neck. The dark penetrating eyes

From "Postscript to a Journey," by José Quintero, in Theatre Arts, XLI *(April, 1957), 27-29, 88. Copyright* © *by Theatre Arts Books, Inc. Reprinted by permission of* Theatre Arts.

were arresting in the steadiness of their gaze. She was dressed in black, which she wore with distinction.

She began to talk about her husband's work, almost as though he were present, as in a sense he was. There were pictures of Eugene O'Neill everywhere. Pictures of him when he was a young, lean, handsome man. Other pictures when pain and anger and frustration had given his eyes a terrifying look. Pictures of Mr. and Mrs. O'Neill taken on their honeymoon in Paris. In the bookcases there were three or four copies of every one of his plays. Mrs. O'Neill talked of his dedication to his work, and how work was the only thing that he really cared about. She asked me a few questions about the Circle in the Square, and I answered them. She rose from her chair and said, "You can do *The Iceman Cometh.*" I left the apartment, almost believing that permission to do the play had come from the dead dramatist himself.

It was less a permission than a sacred charge. *The Iceman Cometh* presented enormous problems at the Circle. It has a cast of twenty, and almost every role is highly complex. The central part of Hickey the salesman, is one of the longest and most difficult in American theatre literature. Where was our little theatre going to get all of those people . . . on so stringently limited a budget? We sent out a casting call and began listening to actors, 100 to 125 a day. After four weeks we had cast all of the characters—with the exception of Hickey. It was an oddly assorted and most unorthodox cast, ranging from highly trained and experienced actors to ones who were beginning their careers at the age of fifty. Some of them had never been in a play before.

The impossible problem remained: We needed a great actor who would be willing to play for $30 a week. That was when Jason Robards, Jr. came into our lives. I had called him, really, with a lesser role in mind, but he insisted on reading a section of Hickey's big speech at the end of the play. (He later told me that he had needed a couple of drinks to make such a demand.)

We had found the impossible. We had found the actor for Hickey.

My approach in directing *The Iceman Cometh* was different from that used in any play I had ever done. It had to be, for this was not built as an orthodox play. It resembles a complex musical form, with themes repeating themselves with slight variation, as melodies do in a symphony. It is a valid device, though O'Neill has often been criticized for it by those who do not see the strength and depth of meaning the repetition achieves.

My work was somewhat like that of an orchestra conductor, emphasizing rhythms, being constantly aware of changing tempos; every character advanced a different theme. The paradox was that for the first time as a director, I began to understand the meaning of precision in drama—and it took a play four and one-half hours long to teach me, a play often criticized as rambling and overwritten.

We rehearsed four weeks and our opening took place on the after-noon of May 8, 1956. We didn't know then, of course, what the critics and the public would think; but at the end of that first performance we, all of us, had a sense of one important success; that a great play had won the right to be revaluated.

Review of the 1956 production of *The Iceman Cometh* by Brooks Atkinson

Since José Quintero's productions at Circle in the Square are always admirable, no one should be surprised by his latest achievement.

But it is impossible not to be excited by his production of Eugene O'Neill's *The Iceman Cometh,* which opened in Mr. Quintero's theatre yesterday. It is a major production of a major theatre work. Taking a long script with a massive theme, Mr. Quintero has succeeded in bringing every part of it alive in the theatre. Although he tells the story simply and spontaneously, he leaves no doubt about the value he places on O'Neill's place in the literature of the stage. Mr. Quintero seems to take him on the level of Ibsen, Strindberg, Gorky, and other modern masters of tragic writing.

If *The Iceman Cometh* seems to belong in Mr. Quintero's theatre, there is a good reason. For Circle in the Square was a night-club originally, and all four of the acts of the O'Neill drama are set in a saloon. The audience has the sensation of participating. The rows of seats are only an extension of David Hayes' setting of the battered, blowzy waterfront saloon and flophouse that is under the fabulous proprietorship of Harry Hope. A few tables and chairs, a squalid bar, a flimsy door leading into the street, a handful of fly-blown chandeliers and a few ranks of benches for the audience—they are all part of the same setting and closely related on that account.

In the circumstances, it is difficult to be objective about this melan-choly, sardonic drama that pulls the rug from under the whole struc-ture of life. It seems, not like something written, but like something that is happening. Although it is terrible in its comment on the need for illusions to maintain an interest in life, it is also comic. Some of the dialogue is pretty funny. On the surface, all the characters are comic, since they live in a world of befuddled fantasy and talk big to compensate for the puniness of their spirits.

Review of the 1956 production of The Iceman Cometh, *by Brooks Atkinson. From* The New York Times, *May 9, 1956. Copyright © 1956 by The New York Times Company. Reprinted by permission of the publisher.*

But beneath them there is nothing more substantial than a void of blackness. These are creatures that once were men—very pungent and picturesque creatures, too, for O'Neill was a good deal of a romantic. But the tone of *The Iceman Cometh* is devastatingly tragic. Life is bearable, it seems to say, only when men contrive not to look at the truth. The performance lasts four and three-quarter hours. For *The Iceman Cometh* is one of the O'Neill marathon dramas. No doubt it could be cut and compressed without destroying anything essential. But as a creative work by a powerful writer, it is entitled to its excesses, which, in fact, may account for the monumental feeling of doom that it pulls down over the heads of the audience.

The performance is a vital one. Mr. Quintero is a versatile conductor who knows how to vary his attack with changes in volume and rhythm; he knows how to orchestrate a performance. In one important respect, this performance surpasses the original of ten years ago. Jason Robards, Jr. plays Hickey, the catalyst in the narrative, like an evangelist. His unction, condescension and piety introduce an element of moral affection that clarifies the perspective of the drama as a whole. His heartiness, his aura of good fellowship give the character of Hickey a feeling of evil mischief it did not have before.

*   *   *

In both the writing and the acting, *The Iceman Cometh* is a mighty theatre work. O'Neill is a giant, and Mr. Quintero is a remarkably gifted artist.

Dudley Nichols on *The Iceman Cometh*

"The iceman of the title is, of course, death," Nichols observed. "I don't think O'Neill ever explained, publicly, what he meant by the use of the archaic word, 'cometh,' but he told me at the time he was writing the play that he meant a combination of the poetic and biblical 'Death cometh'—that is, cometh to all living—and the old bawdy story, a typical Hickey [and Jamie O'Neill] story, of the man who calls upstairs, 'Has the iceman come yet?' and his wife calls back, 'No, but he's breathin' hard.' Even the bawdy story is transformed by the poetic intention of the title, for it is really Death which Hickey's wife, Evelyn, has taken to her breast when she marries Hickey, and her insistence on her great love for Hickey and his undying love for her and her death-like grip on his conscience—her insistence that he *can* change and not

From O'Neill, *by Arthur and Barbara Gelb (New York: Harper & Row, Publishers, 1960), pp. 831-32, 877. Copyright © 1960 by Arthur and Barbara Gelb. Reprinted by permission of the authors.*

get drunk and sleep with whores—is making Death breathe hard on her breast as he approaches ever nearer—as he is about 'to come' in the vernacular sense. It is a strange and poetic intermingling of the exalted and the vulgar, that title."

The truth of the play, as O'Neill explained to Nichols and to two or three other close friends, was that Hickey had long ago begun to harbor a murderous hatred for his wife; she represented his own, punishing conscience.

"God, how Hickey had begun to hate his wife!" said Nichols. "When he gave her a venereal disease, and she forgave him—he wanted to kill her then, deep down in his unconscious. But of course the idea couldn't enter his conscious mind—because he 'loved' her, as she 'loved' him. He'd been on that hop for years. So, when he finally had to kill her, knowing he had to be true to his own nature and go off to Harry's saloon for a shot of Hope, a big drunk and a week with the tarts and bums, he first had to cook another pill of opium and grab the beautiful pipe dream that he was killing her for love—so she wouldn't suffer any longer from his incurable debauchery."

Hickey's delusion vanishes when he discovers that with Evelyn's death he no longer has the desire to go off on a drunk; he is forced to grasp at a new pipe dream—that his release from a guilt-ridden marriage has cleansed him and removed the need for debauchery.

"How fiendishly clever the human mind is!" said Nichols. "When one dream is punctured, when we are finally brought face to face with ourselves or with 'reality,' the mind jumps to another pipe dream and calls it truth—calls it facing reality!"

But Hickey's new pipe dream also vanishes when he discovers that his friends in Harry Hope's saloon will not buy it; they are appalled when they discover he has murdered his wife and regard it as the act of an insane man. Hickey, forced to seize still another illusion, convinces himself that his friends are right—that he is insane.

"I don't see the play as pessimistic," Nichols observed. "It's surely not a gloomy play. O'Neill himself delighted in its laughter. He'd chuckle over the tarts and the others—he loved them all. He didn't feel that the fact that we live largely by illusion is sad. The important thing is to see that we do. The quality of a man is merely the quality of his illusions. We like illusioned people. No happy person lives on good terms with reality. No one has even penetrated what reality is.

*　　*　　*

"Curiously, *The Iceman Cometh,* like any great play, reveals its reviewers more than they reveal the play," Dudley Nichols remarked, on the occasion of the play's successful off-Broadway revival. "All of them complain of its length. Yet they are held by it to the end. What is really at fault is ourselves. We have lost the faculty of sustained attention.

"I use the phrase which Gene used in telling me, years ago, why he was reluctant to have the play produced even the first time. He said we have been conditioned by radio, TV, the movies, advertising, capsule news and a nervous brevity in everything we do, to a point where we have lost the power of sustained attention, which full-bodied works of art demand.

"Unless something moves and jerks, we soon turn away from it. If it doesn't chatter or talk like a machine gun, we don't listen for long. [Walter] Winchell knows this perfectly—he adopted a style which can hold anyone's attention for fifteen minutes and make what he says sound important no matter how trivial it may be. Winchell is a master of the modern style. He is its arch-creator. Joshua Logan catches this style in the theatre; he makes things happen for the eye all the time, no matter whether the play is saying anything or not. Now, a trivial play can be all movement, but a great play cannot. . . .

"The truth is, about *The Iceman Cometh,* all kinds of things are happening all the time, but you have to listen and watch, and you hear repetition because that is the way O'Neill planned it, so that you cannot miss his meaning, and the emotions generated by his drama."

I. A Pair of Negatives

Trying to Like O'Neill

by Eric Bentley

It would be nice to like O'Neill. He is the leading American playwright; damn him, damn all; and damning all is a big responsibility. It is tempting to damn all the rest and make of O'Neill an exception. He *is* an exception in so many ways. He has cared less for temporary publicity than for lasting and deserved fame. When he was successful on Broadway he was not sucked in by Broadway. The others have vanity; O'Neill has self-respect. No dickering with the play doctors in Manhattan hotel rooms. He had the guts to go away and the guts to stay away. O'Neill has always had the grownup writer's concern for that continuity and development which must take place quietly and from within. In a theatre which chiefly attracts idiots and crooks he was a model of good sense and honor.

In 1946 he was raised to the American peerage: his picture was on the cover of *Time* magazine. The national playwright was interviewed by the nationalist press. It was his chance to talk rot and be liked for it. It was his chance to spout optimistic uplift and play the patriotic pundit. O'Neill said:

> I'm going on the theory that the United States, instead of being the most successful country in the world is the greatest failure . . . because it was given everything more than any other country. Through moving as rapidly as it has, it hasn't acquired any real roots. Its main idea is that everlasting game of trying to possess your own soul by the possession of something outside it too. . . .

"Trying to Like O'Neill," by *Eric Bentley. From* In Search of Theater *(New York, Alfred A. Knopf, Inc., 1952), pp. 331-45. Copyright © 1952, 1953 by Eric Bentley. Reprinted by permission of the publisher.*

Henry Luce possesses a good many things besides his own soul. He possesses *Life* as well as *Time,* and in the former he published an editorial complaining of the lack of inspiration to be found in the national playwright. In *The Iceman Cometh* there were no princes and heroes, only bums and drunks. This was "democratic snobbism." Henry Luce was evidently in favor of something more aristocratic (the pin-up girls in his magazine notwithstanding). Inevitably, though, what the aristocrats of *Time Inc.* objected to in O'Neill was his greatest virtue: his ability to stay close to the humbler forms of American life as he had seen them. It is natural that his claim to be a national playwright should rest chiefly on a critical and realistic attitude to American life which they reject. Like the three great Irish playwrights, O'Neill felt his "belonging" to his country so deeply that he took its errors to heart and, although admittedly he wished his plays to be universal, they all start at home; they are specifically a criticism of American life. *Marco Millions* is only the bluntest of his critical studies. Interest in the specifically American pattern of living sustains his lightest work *Ah, Wilderness!* New England patterns are integral to *Desire Under the Elms* and *Mourning Becomes Electra,* the latter being an attempt at an *Oresteia* in terms of American history, with the Civil War as an equivalent of the Trojan War. The protagonist of *The Iceman Cometh* is a product of Hoosier piety, a study much more deeply rooted in American life than Arthur Miller's of a salesman going to his death. It would be nice to like O'Neill because the Luce magazines *dis*like him—that is, because he is opposed to everything they stand for.

Last autumn, when I was invited to direct the German language *première* of *The Iceman,* along with Kurt Hirschfeld, I decided I should actually succeed in liking O'Neill. I reminded myself that he had been honored with prefaces by Joseph Wood Krutch and Lionel Trilling, that he had aroused enthusiasm in the two hardest-to-please of the New York critics, Stark Young and George Jean Nathan, and so forth. I even had a personal motive to aid and abet the pressure of pure reason. My own published strictures on O'Neill had always been taken as a display of gratuitous pugnacity, amusing or reprehensible according to my reader's viewpoint. Under a rain of dissent one begins to doubt one's opinions and to long for the joy that is not confined to heaven when a sinner repenteth. Now it is a fallacy that drama critics are strongly attached to their own opinions; actually they would far rather be congratulated on having the flexibility to change their minds. In short, I would have been glad to write something in praise of O'Neill, and I actually did lecture—and speak on the Swiss radio—as an O'Neillite. If this seems disingenuous, I can only plead that I spoke as a director, not as critic, and that it is sometimes a great relief to do so. There is something too godlike about criticism; it is a defiance of the injunction to men: Judge not that ye be not judged; it is a strain. And if it would be subhuman to give up the critical attitude for mere liking and disliking, the directorial, interpretative attitude seems a more mature and challenging alternative.

Both critic and director are aware of faults, but whereas it is the critic's job to point them out, it is the director's job to cover them up, if only by strongly bringing out a play's merits. It is not true that a director accepts a play with its faults on its head, that he must follow the playwright even into what he believes to be error. He cannot be a self-respecting interpreter without following his own taste and judgment. Thus, Hirschfeld and I thought we were doing our best by O'Neill in toning certain things down and playing others full blast. Specifically, there seemed to us to be in *The Iceman Cometh* a genuine and non-genuine element, the former, which we regarded as the core, being realistic, the latter, which we took as inessential excrescence, being expressionistic. I had seen what came of author-worshipping direction in the Theatre Guild production, where all O'Neill's faults were presented to the public with careful reverence. In order to find the essential—or at least the better—O'Neill we agreed to forego much O'Neillism.

Our designer, Teo Otto, agreed. I told him of Robert Edmond Jones's Rembrandtesque lighting and of the way in which Jones, in his sketches, tried to create the phantasmagoria of a Strindberg dream play, but Otto, though we discussed various sensational ways of setting the play—with slanting floors and Caligari corridors or what not— agreed in the end that we were taking O'Neill's story more seriously if we tried simply to underline the sheer reality, the sheer banality and ugliness, of its locale. Instead of darkness, and dim, soulfully colored lights, we used a harsh white glare, suggesting unshaded electric bulbs in a bare room. And the rooms *were* bare. On the walls Otto suggested the texture of disintegrating plaster: a dripping faucet was their only ornament. A naked girder closed the rooms in from above. And, that this real setting be seen as setting and not as reality itself, the stage was left open above the girder. While Hirschfeld and I were busy avoiding the abstractness of expressionism, Otto made sure that we did not go to the other extreme—a piddling and illusion-mongering naturalism.

To get at the core of reality in *The Iceman*—which is also its artistic, its dramatic core—you have to cut away the rotten fruit of unreality around it. More plainly stated: you have to cut. The play is far too long—not so much in asking that the audience sit there so many hours as on sheer internal grounds. The main story is meant to have suspense but we are suspended so long we forget all about it. One can cut a good many of Larry's speeches since he is forever re-phrasing a pessimism which is by no means hard to understand the first time. One can cut down the speeches of Hugo since they are both too long and too pretentious. It is such a pretentiousness, replete with obvious and unimaginative symbolism, that constitutes the expressionism of the play. Hugo is a literary conception—by Gorky out of Dostoevsky.

We cut about an hour out of the play. It wasn't always easy. Not wishing to cut out whole characters we mutilated some till they had, I'm afraid, no effective existence. But we didn't forget that some of the incidental details of *The Iceman* are among O'Neill's finest achievements. Nothing emerged more triumphantly from our shortened, crisper version than the comic elements. With a dash of good humor O'Neill can do more than with all his grandiloquent lugubriousness. Nothing struck my fancy more, in our production, than the little comedy of the Boer General and the English captain. O'Neill is also very good at a kind of homely genre painting. Harry's birthday party with its cake and candles and the whores singing his late wife's favorite song, "She Is the Sunshine of Paradise Alley," is extremely well done; and no other American playwright could do it without becoming either too sentimental or too sophisticated. We tried to build the scene up into a great theatric image, and were assisted by a magnificent character actor as Harry (Kurt Horwitz). It is no accident that the character of Harry came out so well both in New York and Zurich: the fact is that O'Neill can draw such a man more pointedly than he can his higher flying creations.

I am obviously a biased judge but I think Zurich was offered a more dramatic evening than New York. The abridging of the text did lay bare the main story and release its suspense. We can see the action as presumably we were meant to see it. There is Hickey, and there is Parritt. Both are pouring out their false confessions and professions and holding back their essential secret. Yet, inexorably, though against their conscious will, both are seeking punishment. Their two stories are brought together through Larry Slade whose destiny, in contrast to his intention, is to extract the secret of both protagonists. Hickey's secret explodes, and Larry at last gives Parritt what he wants: a death sentence. The upshot of the whole action is that Larry is brought from a posturing and oratorical pessimism to a real despair. Once the diffuse speeches are trimmed and the minor characters reduced to truly minor proportions, Larry is revealed as the center of the play, and the audience can watch the two stories being played out before him.

A systematic underlining of all that is realistic in the play did, as we hoped it would, bring the locale—Jimmy the Priest's—to successful theatrical realization, despite the deletion of much of O'Neill's detail. It gave body and definition to what otherwise would have remained insubstantial and shapeless; the comedy was sharpened, the sentiment purified. I will not say that the production realized the idea of the play which Hirschfeld, Otto, and I entertained. In theatre there is always too much haste and bungling for that. One can only say that the actuality did not fall further short of the idea in this instance than in others.

And yet it was not a greater success with the public than the New York production, and whereas the New York critics were restrained by awe before the national playwright, the Swiss critics, when they were bored, said so. My newly won liking for O'Neill would perhaps have been unshaken by the general opinion—except that in the end I couldn't help sharing it.

I enjoyed the rehearsal period—unreservedly. I didn't have to conceal my reservations about O'Neill out of tact. They ceased to exist. They were lost in the routine, the tension, and the delight of theatre work. I don't mean to suggest that you could lose yourself thus in any script, however bad; there are scripts that bear down on a director with all the dead weight of their fatuity. But in an O'Neill script there are problems, technical and intellectual, and every one a challenge. I gladly threw myself headlong into that mad joy of the theatre in which the world and its atomic bombs recede and one's own first night seems to be the goal toward which creation strives.

The shock of the first night was the greater. It was not one of those catastrophic first nights when on all faces you can see expectancy fading into ennui or lack of expectancy freezing into a smug I Told You So. But, theatrically speaking, mild approval is little better. Theatrical art is a form of aggression. Like the internal combustion engine it proceeds by a series of explosions. Since it is in the strictest sense the most shocking of the arts, it has failed most utterly when no shock has been felt, and it has failed in a large measure when the shock is mild. *The Iceman* aroused mild interest, and I had to agree that *The Iceman* was only mildly interesting. When I read the critics, who said about my O'Neill production precisely what I as critic had said about other O'Neill productions, my period of liking O'Neill was over.

Of course there were shortcomings which could not be blamed on O'Neill. We were presenting him in German, and in addition to the normal translation problems there were two special ones: that of translating contrasting dialects and that of reproducing the tone of American, semi-gangster, hardboiled talk. There was little the translator could do about the dialects. She wisely did not lay under contribution the various regions of Germany or suggest foreign accents, and her idea of using a good deal of Berlin slang had to be modified for our Swiss public. One simply forewent many of O'Neill's effects or tried to get them by non-verbal means—and by that token one realized how much O'Neill does in the original with the various forms of the

vernacular spoken in New York. One also realizes how much he uses
the peculiarly American institution of Tough Talk, now one of the
conventions of the American stage, a lingo which the young playwright
learns, just as at one time the young poet learned Milton's poetic dic-
tion. In German there seems to be no real equivalent of this lingo because there is no equivalent of the psychology from which it springs
and to which it caters. And there is no teaching the actors how to
speak their lines in the hardboiled manner. Irony is lost, and the
dialogue loses its salt. This loss and that of dialect flavor were undoubtedly great deficiencies. But not the greatest. I saw the production
several times and, in addition to the flaws for which we of the Schau-
spielhaus were responsible, there stood out clearer each time the known,
if not notorious, faults of O'Neill. True, he is a man of the theatre
and, true, he is an eloquent writer composing, as his colleagues on
Broadway usually do not, under the hard compulsion of something he
has to say. But his gifts are mutually frustrating. His sense of theatrical
form is frustrated by an eloquence that decays into mere repetitious
garrulousness. His eloquence is frustrated by the extreme rigidity of the
theatrical mold into which it is poured—jelly in an iron jar. Iron.
Study, for example, the stage directions of *The Iceman,* and you will
see how carefully O'Neill has drawn his ground plan. There everyone
sits—a row of a dozen and a half men. And as they sit, the plot progresses; as each new stage is reached, the bell rings, and the curtain
comes down. Jelly. Within the tyrannically, mechanically rigid scenes,
there is an excessive amount of freedom. The order of speeches can be
juggled without loss, and almost any speech can be cut in half.

The eloquence might of course be regarded as clothing that is necessary to cover a much too mechanical man. Certainly, though we
gained more by abridging the play than we lost, the abridgement did
call attention rather cruelly to the excessively schematic character of
the play. Everything is contrived, *voulu,* drawn on the blackboard,
thought out beforehand, imposed on the material by the dead hand of
calculation. We had started out from the realization that the most lifeless schemata in this over-schematic play are the expressionistic ones
but we had been too sanguine in hoping to conceal or cancel them.
They are foreshadowed already in the table groupings of Act One (as
specified in O'Neill's stage directions). They hold the last act in a
death grip. Larry and Parritt are on one side shouting their duet.
Hickey is in the center singing his solo. And at the right, arranged
en bloc, is everyone else, chanting their comments in what O'Neill
himself calls a "chorus."

It would perhaps be churlish to press the point, were O'Neill's ambition in this last act not symptomatic both of his whole endeavor
as a playwright and of the endeavor of many other serious playwrights

in our time. It is the ambition to transcend realism. O'Neill spoke of
it nearly thirty years ago in a note on Strindberg:

> It is only by means of some form of "super-naturalism" that we may
> express in the theatre what we comprehend intuitively of that self-
> obsession which is the particular discount we moderns have to pay for the
> loan of life. The old naturalism—or realism if you will (I wish to God
> some genius were gigantic enough to define clearly the separateness of
> these terms once and for all!) —no longer applies. It represents our fathers'
> daring aspirations towards self-recognition by holding the family kodak
> up to ill-nature. But to us their audacity is blague, we have taken too
> many snapshots of each other in every graceless position. We have endured
> too much from the banality of surfaces.

So far, so good. This is only a warning against that extreme and narrow form of realism generally known as naturalism. Everyone agrees.
The mistake is only to talk as if it followed that one must get away
from realism altogether, a mistake repeated by every poetaster who
thinks he can rise above Ibsen by writing flowerily (e.g. Christopher
Fry as quoted and endorsed by *Time* magazine). Wherever O'Neill
tries to clarify his non-realistic theory the only thing that is clear is
lack of clarity. For example:

> It was far from my idea in writing *The Great God Brown* that the back-
> ground pattern of conflicting tides in the soul of man should ever over-
> shadow and thus throw out of proportion the living drama of the recog-
> nizable human beings. . . . I meant *it* always to be mystically within
> and behind them, giving them a significance beyond themselves, forcing
> itself through them to expression in mysterious words, symbols, actions
> they do not themselves comprehend. And that is as clearly as I wish an
> audience to comprehend *it*. *It* is Mystery—the mystery any one man or
> woman can feel but not understand as the meaning of any event—or
> accident—in any life on earth. And it is this mystery which I want to
> realize in the theatre.

I have italicized the word *it* to underline the shift in reference that
takes place. The first two times "it" is "the background pattern of conflicting tides in the soul of man." The third time "it" is just a blur,
meaning nothing in particular, exemplifying rather than clearing up
the mystery which O'Neill finds important. An event can be mysterious,
but how can its mystery be its meaning? And how can we know that its
mystery is its meaning if we do "not understand" it? And what would
constitute a "realization" of such a phenomenon in the theatre?

In a letter to Thomas [sic] Hobson Quinn, O'Neill tries again. He
has been seeking to be a poet, he says,

> and to see the transfiguring nobility of tragedy, in as near the Greek
> sense as one can grasp it, in seemingly the most ignoble, debased lives.

And just here is where I am a most confirmed mystic too, for I'm always, always trying *to interpret Life in terms of lives, never just lives in terms of characters.* I'm always acutely conscious of the Force behind (Fate, God, our biological past creating our present, whatever one calls it— Mystery certainly) and of the one eternal tragedy of Man in his glorious, self-destructive struggle *to make the Force express him instead of being, as an animal is, an infinitesimal incident in its expression.* And my profound conviction is that this is the only subject worth writing about and that it is possible—or can be—to develop [syntax?] a tragic expression in terms of transfigured modern values and symbols in the theatre which may to some degree bring home to members of a modern audience their ennobling identity with the tragic figures on the stage. Of course, this is very much of a dream, but where theatre is concerned, one must have a dream and the Greek dream in tragedy is the noblest ever!

I have italicized this time phrases where we expect O'Neill to say something, where we even think for a moment that he *has* said something. Reading them several times over, we find that we could give them a meaning—but without any assurance that it is O'Neill's. What is interpreting "Life in terms of lives" and what is "mystical" about it? What does it mean to be "expressed" by a Force—as against being an incident in "its expression"? Isn't O'Neill comforting himself with verbiage? For what connection is there—beyond the external ones of *Mourning Becomes Electra*—between his kind of drama and the Greek? How could one be ennobled by identifying oneself with any of his characters?

It is no use wanting to get away from realism (or anything else) unless you know what you want to get away *to*. Raising a dust of symbols and poeticisms is not to give artistic expression to a sense of mystery. It is merely, in O'Neill's case, to take your eye off the object. (Cf. Ibsen: "To be a poet is chiefly to see.") It seems to me that O'Neill's eye was off the object, and on Dramatic and Poetic Effects, when he composed the Hickey story. Not being clearly seen, the man is unclearly presented to the audience: O'Neill misleads them for several hours, then asks them to reach back into their memory and re-interpret all Hickey's actions and attitudes from the beginning. Is Hickey the character O'Neill needed as the man who tries to deprive the gang of their illusions? He (as it turns out) is a maniac. But if the attempt to disillude the gang is itself mad, it would have more dramatic point made by a sane idealist (as in *The Wild Duck*).

Does O'Neill find the meaning of his story by looking at the people and the events themselves or by imposing it on them? There are ideas in the play, and we have the impression that what should be the real substance of it is mere (not always deft) contrivance to illustrate the ideas. The main ideas are two: first the one we have touched on, that people may as well keep their illusions; second, that one should not hate and punish but love and forgive. The whole structure of the play is so inorganic, it is hardly to be expected that the two ideas would be organically related. The difficulty is in finding what relation they do have. In a way the truth-illusion theme is a red herring, and, as in *Cosi è* (*se vi pare*), the author's real interest is in the love-hate theme. Pirandello, however, presents the red herring *as* a red herring, relates his "false" theme to this real one. O'Neill is unclear because he fails to do so. A high official of the Theatre Guild remarked: "the point is, you aren't *meant* to understand." In Pirandello this is indeed the point of the Ponza/Frola story. Pirandello *makes* the point, and in art a point has to be made before it can be said to exist. For O'Neill it is merely a point he might have made. As things are, it is his play, and not life, that is unintelligible.

The Iceman, of course, has big intentions written all over it. Most of O'Neill's plays have big intentions written all over them. He has written of

> the death of an old God and the failure of science and materialism to give any satisfying new one for the surviving primitive religious instinct to find a meaning for life in, and to comfort its fears of death with. It seems to me [he adds] anyone trying to do big work nowadays must have this subject behind all the little subjects of his plays or novels.

In other words, O'Neill's intentions as a writer are no less vast than Dostoevsky's. *The Iceman* is his version of crime and punishment. What is surprising is not that his achievements fall below Dostoevsky's but that critics—including some recent rehabilitators—have taken the will for the deed and find O'Neill's "nobler conception" of theatre enough. "Conception" is patently a euphemism for "intention" and they are applauding O'Neill for strengthening the pavement of hell. In this they are not disingenuous; their own intentions are also good; they are simply a party to a general gullibility. People believe what they are told, and in our time a million units of human energy are spent on the telling to every one that is spent on examining what is told; reason is swamped by propaganda and publicity. Hence it is that an author's professions and intentions, broadcast not only by himself but by an army of interested and even disinterested parties, determine what people think his work is. The realm of false culture thus created is not all on one level; brows here, as elsewhere, may be low or high. No brows are higher indeed than those of the upper stratum of the subintelligentsia. They spend their time seeking sublimities, works which provide the answers to the crying questions of our time, impassioned appeals for justice, daring indictments of tyranny, everything surefire. Seek and you shall find: a writer like O'Neill does not give them the optimism of an "American century" but he provides profunndities galore, and technical innovations, and (as he himself says) Mystery. Now there is a large contingent of the subintelligentsia in the theatre world. They are seen daily at the Algonquin and nightly at Sardi's. They don't all like O'Neill, yet his "profound" art is inconceivable without them. O'Neill doesn't like *them,* but he needs them, and could never have dedicated himself to "big work" had their voices not been in his ears telling him he was big. The man who could not be bribed by the Broadway tycoons was seduced by the Broadway intelligentsia.

At one time he performed a historic function, that of helping the American theatre to grow up. In all his plays an earnest attempt is made to interpret life; this fact in itself places O'Neill above his predecessors in American drama and beside his colleagues in the novel and poetry. He was a good playwright insofar as he kept within the somewhat narrow range of his own sensibility. When he stays close to a fairly simple reality and when, by way of technique, he uses fairly simple forms of realism or fairly simple patterns of melodrama, he can render the bite and tang of reality or, alternatively, he can startle and stir us with his effects. If he is never quite a poet, he is occasionally able—as we have seen in *The Iceman*—to create the striking theatric image.

But the more he attempts, the less he succeeds. *Lazarus Laughed* and *The Great God Brown* and *Days Without End* are inferior to *The Emperor Jones* and *Anna Christie* and *Ah, Wilderness!.* O'Neill has never learned this lesson. The idea of "big work" lured him out into territory where his sensibility is entirely inoperative. Even his most ardent admirers have little to say in favor of *Dynamo,* the only play where he frontally assails the problem of "the death of an old God and the failure of science." A hundred novelists have dealt more subtly with hidden motives than O'Neill did in his famous essay in psychological subtlety, *Strange Interlude,* a play which is equally inferior as a study of upper-class Americans. Then there is his desire to re-create ancient tragedy. Though no one is more conscious than he that America is not an Athens, the "Greek dream"—the desire to be an Aeschylus—has been his nightmare.

The classic and notorious problem about tragedy in modern dress has been that the characters, not being over life-size but rather below it, excite pity without admiration and therefore without terror. Though O'Neill has talked of an "ennobling identification" with protagonists, he has only once tried to do anything about it: only in *Mourning Becomes Electra* are the characters over life-size. Unhappily this is not because of the size of their bones but, as it were, by inflation with gas, cultural and psychological.

The cultural gas is the classic story. The use of classic stories has been customary for so long, and has recently come into such vogue again, that writers have forgotten their obligation to make the stories their own. They figure that the Aeschylean names will themselves establish the dignity and identity of the subject, while they —the modern adaptors—get the credit and draw the royalties. They are not necessarily conscious opportunists. They probably assume, with some psychologists and anthropologists, that archetypal patterns of myth elicit profound responses of themselves, irrespective of presentation; if this were true the poet would be unnecessary; it is a belief not to be discussed by a critic since the very act of criticism presupposes its falsity. If we ask what difference it makes that Orin and Lavinia are versions of Orestes and Electra the answer is that they thereby acquire an artificial prestige. They have become more important without any creative work on the author's part. We now associate them with the time-honored and sublime. They are inflated with cultural gas. It's like finding out that your girl friend is the daughter of a duke. If you are impressionable, you are impressed; she will seem different from now on, clad in all your illusions about nobility.

We are told that myth is useful because the audience knows the plot already and can turn its attention to the how and why. To this I would not protest that all adaptors, including O'Neill, change the mythic plots, though this is true; what I have in mind is, rather, that they do not always change them enough. Events in their works have often no organic place there, they are fossilized vestiges of the older version. We ask: why does this character do that? And the answer is: because his Greek prototype did it. In *Mourning Becomes Electra* the myth makes it hard for O'Neill to let his people have their own identity at all, yet to the extent that they do have one, it is, naturally, a modern and American identity, and this in turn makes their ancient and Greek actions seem wildly improbable. Heaven knows that murders take place today as in ancient times; but the murders in O'Neill are not given today's reality.

Instead, the characters are blown up with psychological gas. O'Neill has boasted his ignorance of Freud but such ignorance is not enough. He should be ignorant also of the watered-down Freudianism of Sardi's and the Algonquin, the Freudianism of all those who are ignorant of Freud, the Freudianism of the subintelligentsia. It is through this Freudianism, and through it alone, that O'Neill has made the effort, though a vain one, to assimilate the myth to modern life. Now what is it that your subintellectual knows about Freud? That he "put everything down to sex." Precisely; and that is what O'Neill does with the myth. Instead of reverent family feeling to unite an Orestes and an Electra we have incest. *Mourning Becomes*

Electra is all sex talk. Sex *talk*—not sex lived and embodied but sex talked of and fingered. The sex talk of the subintelligentsia. It is the only means by which some sort of eloquence and urgency gets into the play, the source of what is meant to be its poetry. The Civil War never gains the importance it might have had in this telling of the story, it is flooded out by sex. "New England," surely a cultural conception with wider reference than this, stands only, in O'Neill, for the puritanic (i.e. sexually repressive) attitude.

O'Neill is an acute case of what Lawrence called "sex in the head." Sex is almost the only idea he has—has insistently—and it is for him *only* an idea. Looking back on what I wrote about him a few years ago, I still maintain that O'Neill is no thinker. He is so little a thinker, it is dangerous for him to think. To prove this you have only to look at the fruits of his thinking; his comparatively thoughtless plays are better. For a non-thinker he thinks too much.

Almost as bad as sex in the head is tragedy in the head, for tragedy too can decline into a doctrine and dwindle into an idea. And when the thing is absent its "idea" is apt to go soft. Tragedy is hard, but the idea of tragedy ("the tragic view of life," "the tragic sense of life" etc.) is seldom evoked without nostalgic longing. And the most decadent longing is the longing for barbarism, *nostalgie de la boue,* such as is voiced by our tragedy-loving poets:

> Poetry is not a civilizer, rather the reverse, for great poetry appeals to the most primitive instincts. . . . Tragedy has been regarded, ever since Aristotle, as a moral agent, a purifier of the mind and emotions. But the story of *Medea* is about a criminal adventurer and his gun-moll; it is no more moral than the story of Frankie and Johnny; only more ferocious. And so with the yet higher summits of Greek Tragedy, the *Agamemnon* series and the *Oedipus Rex*; they all tell primitive horror stories, and the conventional pious sentiments of the chorus are more than balanced by the bad temper and wickedness, or folly, of the principal characters. What makes them noble is the poetry; the poetry and the beautiful shapes of the plays, and the extreme violence born of extreme passion. . . . These are stories of disaster and death, and it is not in order to purge the mind of passions but because death and disaster are exciting. People love disaster, if it does not touch them too nearly—as we run to see a burning house or a motor crash. . . .

Aristotle's view of tragedy is humane, this one—that of Robinson Jeffers—is barbaric without the innocence of barbarism; it is neo-barbaric, decadent. O'Neill is too simple and earnest to go all the way with Jeffers. Puritanism and a rough-hewn honesty keep him within the realm of the human. But *Mourning Becomes Electra* does belong, so to speak, to the same world as Jeffers' remarks, a world which titillates itself with tragedy in the head. Your would-be tragedian despises realism, the problem play, liberalism, politics in general, optimism, and what not. Hence *Mourning Becomes Electra* is unrealistic, unsocial, illiberal, unpolitical, and pessimistic. What of the *Oresteia?* It celebrates the victory of law over arbitrary violence, of the community over the individual. It is optimistic, political, social and with permissible license might be called liberal and realistic as well. *O tempora, o mores!*

If one does not like O'Neill, it is not really he that one dislikes: it is our age—of which like the rest of us he is more the victim than the master.

Eugene O'Neill—Dry Ice

by Mary McCarthy

The crucial figure of O'Neill's new play is a mad hardware salesman. Consonantly, the play itself is like some stern piece of hardware
in one of those dusty old-fashioned stores into which no Pyrex dish or
herb shelf or French provincial earthenware had yet penetrated, which
dealt in iron-colored enamel, galvanized tin, lengths of pipe and
wrenches, staples, saws, and nails, and knew nothing more sophisticated than the double boiler. Ugly, durable, mysteriously utilitarian,
this work gives the assurance that it has been manufactured by a re-
liable company; it is guaranteed to last two-and-a-half hours longer
than any other play, with the exception of the uncut *Hamlet.*

The Iceman Cometh is indeed made of ice or iron; it is full of will
and fanatic determination; it appears to have hardened at some extreme temperature of the mind. In the theatre today, it is attractive
positively because of its defects. To audiences accustomed to the oily
virtuosity of George Kaufman, George Abbott, Lillian Hellman,
Odets, Saroyan, the return of a playwright who—to be frank—cannot
write is a solemn and sentimental occasion. O'Neill belongs to that
group of American authors, which includes Farrell and Dreiser, whose
choice of vocation was a kind of triumphant catastrophe; none of
these men possessed the slightest ear for the word, the sentence, the
speech, the paragraph; all of them, however, have, so to speak, en-
forced the career they decreed for themselves by a relentless policing
of their beat. What they produce is hard to praise or to condemn; how
is one to judge the great, logical symphony of a tone-deaf musician?
Pulpy in detail, their work has nevertheless a fine solidity of structure;
they drive an idea or a theme step by step to its brutal concluion with
the same terrible force they have brought to bear on their profession.
They are among the few contemporary American writers who know
how to exhaust a subject; that is, alas, their trouble. Their logical,
graceless works can find no reason for stopping, but go on and on, like
elephants pacing in a zoo. In their last acts and chapters, they arrive

"Eugene O'Neill—Dry Ice," by Mary McCarthy. From Sights and Spectacles (*New
York: Farrar, Straus, & Giroux, 1956), pp. 81-85. Copyright 1937 by Mary McCarthy.
Reprinted by permission of the publisher.*

not at despair but at a strange, blank nihilism. Their heroes are all
searchers; like so many non-verbal, inarticulate people, they are looking for a final Word that will explain everything. These writers are,
naturally, masters of suspense.

O'Neill has neither the phenomenal memory which serves Farrell
as a substitute for observation, nor the documentary habits which, for
Dreiser, performed the same service. In *The Iceman Cometh*, the scene
is a cheap bar somewhere in downtown New York in the year 1912;
the characters are the derelict habitués of the back room—a realist's
paradise, one would think. But it needs only a short walk along Third
Avenue today (or the armchair method of inquiry) to solidify the suspicion that, unless drinking *moeurs* have changed in the last thirty-
five years, O'Neill is an incompetent reporter. In the day and a half
that elapses on the stage of the Martin Beck, none of the characters is
visibly drunk, nobody has a hangover, and, with a single brief exception, nobody has the shakes; there are none of those rancorous, semi-
schizoid silences, no obscurity of thought, no dark innuendoes, no
flashes of hatred, there is, in short, none of the terror of drink, which,
after all, in the stage that Harry Hope's customers have presumably
reached, is a form of insanity. What is missing is precisely the thing
that is most immediately striking and most horrifying in any human
drunkard, the sense of the destruction of personality. Each of O'Neill's
people is in perfect possession of the little bit of character the author
has given him. The Boer is boerish, the Englishman english, the philosopher philosophizes, and the sentimental grouch who runs the establishment grouches and sentimentalizes in orderly alternation. So
obedient indeed are these supposed incorrigibles to the play's thematic
dictation, so well behaved in speech and in silence, that one might
imagine, if one shut one's eyes, that one was attending the Christmas
exercises in some respectable school ("I am Wind, I blow and blow,"
says little Aeolus with his bag).

And the didactic tone is, in fact, the play's natural mode. The "realistic" scene that stretches, rather Moscow Art style and friezelike,
across the stage is no more than mood or *décor*. The play quickly calls
itself to order, the drunkards awake and embark on an elementary
study of the nature of reality and illusion. Each drunkard, it seems,
has his "pipe-dream": he imagines that tomorrow he will get a job,
take a walk, marry, see the anarchist millennium, go home to England
or South Africa. A hardware salesman, beloved of all, who is expected
to arrive for one of his periodical benders, finally does appear on the
dot of the dramatist's excellent schedule; he is changed, sober, exhila-
rated, he has a mission to perform; he will cure Harry Hope and his
customers of the illusions that are making them unhappy. In the
course of the play, he obliges each of the characters to test himself.

All fail to carry out the actions projected in the pipe-dream, but self-knowledge, the recognition of failure, does not bring them the freedom the salesman promised. On the contrary, it kills whatever life was left in them; disgruntled, despairing, demoralized, they cannot even get drunk, though they are full of red-eye whiskey. Fortunately, it turns out that the salesman had attained his own state of freedom and euphoria by killing his wife; the police come for him, and Harry Hope and his clients, perceiving that he is mad, can dismiss the truths he has taught them and feel their liquor again (though this statement must be taken on faith, since here, as in the rest of the play, alcoholism does not have its customary sour breath, and the characters, like the actors who are impersonating them, seem to have been swallowing ponies of tea). As the happy derelicts carouse, one character who is without illusions, the boy who has betrayed his anarchist mother to the police, goes out and commits suicide, and another character, the philosopher, who is also capable of facing truth, indicates that he will soon join him in a plunge from the fire-escape. Life, then, consists of illusion, and if death is reality, reality is also death.

The odd thing about *The Iceman Cometh* is that this rather bony synopsis does it perfect justice; in fact, it improves it by substituting, whenever possible, the word *illusion* for the word *pipe-dream,* which recurs with a crankish and verbally impoverished tastefulness about two hundred times during the play. What shreds of naturalism cling to this work are attached to and encumber the dialogue; the language has the wooden verisimilitude, the flat, dead, echoless sound of stale slang that makes Farrell's novels and the later works of Sinclair Lewis so stilted. O'Neill here has not even the justification of sociological pedantry, which these other writers might bring forward. His intention is symbolic and philosophical, but unfortunately you cannot write a Platonic dialogue in the style of *Casey at the Bat.* O'Neill might have studied the nature of illusion through the separate relations to illusion of a group of characters (*The Three Sisters*), but his people are given but a single trait each, and they act and react, in the loss and recapture of illusion, not individually but in a body. Bare and plain, this play has the structure of an argument; its linguistic deficiencies make it maudlin. How is your wife getting along with the iceman, the characters roar, over and over again, and though death is the iceman, the joke is not appreciably refined by this symbolic treatment; rather, it is death that is coarsened.

Yet it must be said for O'Neill that he is probably the only man in the world who is still laughing at the iceman joke or pondering its implications. He is certainly the only writer who would have the courage or the lack of judgment to build a well-made play around it. This sense of one man's isolation is what, above all, gives *The Iceman*

Cometh its salient look. Though it is full of reminders of Saroyan (the barroom, the loose-witted philosophical talk, the appearance of the Redeemer at the middle table), of O'Casey (again the drunkards, and the tense, frightened young man who has betrayed the Cause), of Ibsen, Thornton Wilder, and even of Maxwell Anderson (the ripples of the Mooney and Sacco-Vanzetti cases which lap at the edges of a distant slum, and again the home-made philosophy) *The Iceman Cometh* seems nevertheless estranged from all influences and impressions. Its solitariness inside its rigid structure suggests the prison or the asylum or the sound of a man laughing in a square, empty room.

II. *The Iceman Cometh* AS HISTORY AND BIOGRAPHY

The Historical Background of
The Iceman Cometh

by John Henry Raleigh

O'Neill's finest histories [historical plays] are autobiographies as well, and take place in the "remembered" past, in the early twentieth century: *Ah, Wilderness!*, *The Iceman Cometh*, *A Long Day's Journey Into Night*, *A Moon for the Misbegotten*, and *Hughie*. Even though O'Neill never completed his consciously planned cycle of plays on American history, he did nevertheless, albeit unconsciously, finally leave an "American" cycle if we look at the nineteenth- and twentieth-century American plays as an historical unit and sequence, despite the fact that only in *Long Day's Journey Into Night* and *A Moon for the Misbegotten* is there a carry-over of characters. The sequence would cover exactly one century, from *A Touch of the Poet* (1828) to *Hughie* (1928), from the era of Adams-Jackson to that of Hoover. The historical character of most of these plays is underlined by the fact that they seldom take place in a vacuum. The Adams-Jackson presidential contest is as integral to the background of *A Touch of the Poet* as the Great Depression is to *Hughie*. Even the apolitical and asocial *Long Day's Journey* and *A Moon for the Misbegotten* remind us, if ever so slightly, of the existence of, and the wealth of, the Standard Oil Company.

The twentieth-century plays in the historical category divide themselves into the directly autobiographical, *Long Day's Journey* and *A Moon for the Misbegotten*, about O'Neill and his family; the obliquely autobiographical, *Ah, Wilderness!*, based on a family the O'Neills knew in New London; *The Iceman Cometh*, dealing with characters O'Neill knew in his down-and-out days in New York; and *Hughie*. (I do not know, nor does any student of O'Neill as yet, so far as I know,

"*The Historical Background of* The Iceman Cometh," *by John Henry Raleigh. From* The Plays of Eugene O'Neill (*Carbondale, Ill.: Southern Illinois University Press, 1965), pp. 66-75. Copyright* © *1965 by Southern Illinois University Press. Reprinted by permission of the publisher.*

54

the living sources for the characters and conceptions in the last. If such exist I suppose some day a scholar will identify them.) If sorrow envelopes *Long Day's Journey* and *A Moon for the Misbegotten* and pathos is the note of *Hughie,* it is nostalgia that envelopes *Ah, Wilderness!* and, less obviously and less inconclusively, *The Iceman Cometh.* The various tragedies, and the themes, of *The Iceman Cometh* are so bleak that as the humor of the play is almost completely overlooked, so its nostalgic elements are set aside or unremarked. Yet *The Iceman Cometh* is, in part, a companion piece for *Ah, Wilderness!,* looking back from the middle of the twentieth century at pre-World War I America and seeing it through the indulgent, but not falsifying, haze of nostalgia. Nostalgia is the only kind of sentimentality that is honest and, in the later plays, this is the only sentimentality in which O'Neill indulged.

The nostalgic element in *The Iceman Cometh* is rather complicated by the fact that, though the time of the play is 1912, the characters are practically all living in the past, in most cases a long-ago past; so that the nostalgia is really about the late nineteenth century. Larry, for example, had left "The Movement" (anarchism) eleven years before, or in 1901, but he had been in it for thirty years, which means he joined it in 1871. Harry Hope had not been out of his saloon for twenty years, or since 1892. The song sung in Acts I and II, "She's the Sunshine of Paradise Alley" (the melody of which was taken from Mascagni's *Cavalleria Rusticana*), about which Cora exclaims, "I've forgotten dat has-been tune," was composed by Walter H. Ford and John W. Bratton and became popular in 1895.[1] The Boer War, which figures so prominently in the memories and motivations of Wetjoen and Lewis, took place in 1899-1902. Hickey's story of his life—the forty-five minute monologue that forms the climax of the play—has, in great part, nineteenth-century America for its backdrop since he is about fifty and therefore must have been born around 1862. In fact about the only way that the America of 1912 gets into the play is in references to the I.W.W. and to "de Bull Moosers" mentioned in Act I by Margie and Pearl, and the bombing in which Parritt's mother was involved. But the New York that Joe, Harry, and the other New Yorkers remember and dote upon is the good old days—"Dem old days!"—richly, unashamedly corrupt, automobile-less, peopled with such giants as Richard Croker, "Big Tim" Sullivan, John L. Sullivan, and Jim Corbett, whose framed photographs are seen over the mirror behind the bar in Act III, and with Harry's termagant wife, now deceased, transformed into a loving spouse. Even the fall of Oban's father, the King of the Bucket Shops, must go back five years or so to 1907. Bucket

[1] For my information about American popular music I am relying on Sigmund Spaeth's invaluable *A History of Popular Music in America* (New York, 1948).

shops, which first came into existence after the Civil War, were sham stockbrokerages which really gambled in the stock market. Their first big heyday was from 1900 to 1907. A financial panic wiped them out in 1907, but they had their greatest, and final, resurgence from 1917 to 1929.

In other words, the days most of the New Yorkers are talking about are those of the 1890's, one of the most flourishing periods of Tammany Hall [2] when Richard Croker, the most autocratic and ruthless of the Tammany bosses and the one who dominated the organization from 1886 to 1902, had corruption organized on a hitherto unparalleled scale. "Big Tim" Sullivan, also known as "The Big Feller," was the political boss of the Sixth District of Manhattan, the East Side below Fourteenth Street, but he was such a power in Tammany itself that he was one of the real leaders of the organization as a whole, so much so that no one could be the boss of Tammany without his consent and support. The conjunction of the two prize fighters, John L. Sullivan and Jim Corbett, with the two politicians, Croker and Sullivan, was not fortuitous, for both Croker and Sullivan were known for, and got their political start with, their prowess with their fists; in the "good old days" this was how an aspiring young politician first made his mark.

By 1912, when *The Iceman Cometh* takes place, Croker had long since retired from the scene, and in that year "Big Tim" Sullivan went insane and was confined. Sullivan, whatever his sins and they were many, up to and including the direction of organized crime, was one of the most colorful and likable of the old leaders and was, in fact, the last of the important "old-style" leaders, who kept a saloon, knew everybody personally, led parades, provided Thanksgiving and Christmas dinners for the poor, had a taste for public sentiment and melo-

[2] The literature on Tammany Hall is considerable and tends to verge into two extremes, whitewash and diatribe; the diatribe is preponderant and rightly so. As James Bryce said about Tammany: "The phenomena of municipal democracy in the United States are the most remarkable and least laudable which the modern world has witnessed; and they present some evils which no political philosopher, however unfriendly to popular government, appears to have foreseen, evils which have scarcely showed themselves in the cities of Europe, and unlike those which were thought characteristic of the rule of the masses in ancient times" (*The American Commonwealth* [New York, 1913], II, 379). The two most comprehensive histories, both in scope and documentation, of Tammany Hall are those of Gustavus Myers, *The History of Tammany Hall* (New York, 1901; revised, 1917); and M. R. Werner, *Tammany Hall* (New York, 1928). I am relying on these two books for my facts. The most interesting "inside" document is W. R. Riordon's *Plunkitt of Tammany Hall* (New York, 1948). George Washington Plunkitt was a district leader, like Sullivan, although not nearly so powerful, who in a series of conversations explained his "philosophy of government" to a newspaper reporter, William Riordon, who first published these conversations in 1905.

drama, and so on.[3] The year 1912 also witnessed the notorious Blumenthal murder which publicly exposed New York police corruption and eventuated in the setting up of a commission, the Curran Committee of the Board of Aldermen, to investigate the police. At least one old-time New York "character," "Big Dick" Butler, thought that 1912 marked the real end of the "good old days."[4] Since 1902 the boss of Tammany had been Charles Murphy, sometimes known as "Sir Charles" or "Charles I," a closemouthed man who lived on a dignified estate on Long Island, complete with a nine-hole golf course. While in town he could be met, by those he really wanted to see, only by his summons to a luxurious suite on the second floor of Delmonico's restaurant. At the Hall he was seen by those who requested to see him. Since the décor of the establishment at Delmonico's was red, it was known as "The Scarlet Room of Mystery." With reference to Murphy's previous life as a ward leader, Gustavus Meyers remarked: "Mr. Murphy's habits as a leader at this time were in singular contrast with those of years previously when, as a district leader, he had made his hailing place a lamp post. He now used a luxurious suite of rooms at Delmonico's fashionable restaurant" (p. 355). The mayors of New York at this time, the first decade of the twentieth century, were by and large respectable. The most important change in Tammany was that some of the visitors to "The Scarlet Room of Mystery" were powerful

[3] On October 31, 1909, "Big Tim" Sullivan made his only public speech, touching on experiences and sentiments which made up the apologia of James Tyrone in Act IV of *Long Day's Journey Into Night*. It was the end of a bitter political campaign, and Tammany and Sullivan had been subjected to many charges of corruption. Miner's Theatre, which Sullivan owned, was engaged for the occasion, and to a full house, with tears running down his pink cheeks, "Big Tim" made his justificatory speech for himself and for the Tammany-type politician. It was a masterpiece of melodrama and sentiment and not without a good deal of truth. Its key passage was just like the key passage of James Tyrone's account in *Long Day's Journey* about his childhood; in fact, the two situations were identical as to the number of children involved (six), the absence of a father, and the sweet, martyr-like mother: "I was born in poverty, one of six children, four boys and two girls. The boys used to sleep in a three-quarters bed, not big enough for two, and the girls in a shakedown on the floor. Some nights there was enough to eat and some nights there wasn't. And our old mother used to sing to us at night and maybe it would be the next day before we would think she had been singing but that she had gone to bed without anything to eat.

"That's the kind of people we come from, and that is the kind of mothers that bore us down here. If we can help some boy or some father to another chance we are going to give it to them" (Werner, p. 503). It would be tempting to think that Eugene O'Neill had heard, or heard of, this speech, but he had left New York for Honduras in early October 1909.

[4] Richard J. Butler and Joseph Driscoll, *Dock Walloper* (New York, 1933): "I was one of those mourners when the crêpe-hanging reformers began getting the upper hand. The wide-open town was killed in 1912, when the Becker-Blumenthal scandal broke, . . ." (p. 112).

and respectable, nominally anyway, financiers and businessmen with whom Murphy carried on business within the law. In short, the façade of Tammany had become respectable and many of its dealings had the odor of sanctity, because, as M. R. Werner says, Murphy taught Tammany that "more money could be made by a legal contract than by petty blackmail" (p. 557). Not that Tammany's connections with vice and corruption had disappeared by 1912; to the contrary they flourished, but in a more discreet, less open, fashion. (Police corruption had in fact actually been curtailed somewhat, in the large sense.) Twice in *The Iceman Cometh* McGloin, who had been thrown off the Police Force in "the good old days" for being *too* greedy, speaks longingly of what is going on in the "reformed" present: "Man alive, from what the boys tell me, there's sugar galore these days" (II). And Rocky must pay the police to protect his two tarts, Pearl and Margie. Still, as Larry says to Parritt in his characterization of McGloin in Act I, McGloin's day was "back in the flush times of graft when everything went." Then when the usual reform investigation came, McGloin was caught red-handed and thrown off the Police Force. After describing McGloin, Larry nods at Joe Mott and remarks that Mott had "a yesterday in the same flush period. He ran a colored gambling house."

Through Mott's reminiscences in Act I we have a concrete vignette of what the flush period was like, as he describes how he was permitted to set up his gambling house. He had saved his money and had gotten a letter to "de Big Chief" from Harry, who at that time was a minor Tammanyite and knew the Chief. "De Big Chief" in the play is called "Big Bill," but in reality it must have been "Big Tim" Sullivan, whose special province was control of gambling and gambling houses during the Croker period.[5] Of the physical size of "de Chief" there can be no doubt, for Joe Mott dwells on it: sitting down, "big as a freight train"; standing up, "big as two freight trains"; and with a fist "like a ham." He roars at Joe to scare him and then gives quiet permission to open, and, as Joe says, "I run wide open for years." For the flush times were the years of the magic "word": no laws, documents, or formal agreements, just the personal say-so from the right person. As McGloin puts it in Act III: "All I've got to do is see the right ones and get them to pass the word. They will, too. They know I was framed. And once they've passed the word, it's as good as done, law or no law." Harry himself was once, in Larry's phrase, a "jitney Tammany politician" whom in 1892, the year of Bessie's death, "the boys" were going to nominate for Alderman: "It was all fixed" (I). Almost immediately though, and in characteristic *Iceman Cometh* fash-

[5] Sullivan, Frank Farrell, the leading professional gambler of the day, and William S. Devery, Chief of Police of New York, ran the gambling syndicate (Werner, p. 416).

ion, it is suggested that "the boys" were going to run him only because they knew they were going to lose the ward anyway. Still, Harry had once known the right people, as Joe Mott attests; and, as the general stage directions say, he still possesses friends, sufficiently so for him to evade the technicalities of present-day laws, such as the Raines Law.

The Raines Law itself is one other roadblock that stands between Harry Hope's saloon and the good old days. The implication generally, in the reminiscences of Harry, Joe Mott, Mosher, McGloin, and some of the others, is that in the 1890's Harry Hope's saloon was a relatively prosperous place; as Joe Mott says, "Dis was a first-class hangout for sports in dem days" (I). Most aspiring Tammany politicians had gotten their start not only because of their fistical prowess but by running a saloon, as had "Big Tim" Sullivan; hence the talk of running Harry for alderman of the ward, a small affair but a not at all impossible post for the well-liked owner of a "first-class hangout for sports." But in 1912 Harry Hope's saloon is decayed, seedy, the tavern of the lost, and is described by O'Neill as having become a "Raines Law hotel of the period."

The Raines Law,[6] so called after the prohibitionist Senator Raines, who was its sponsor, was passed by the New York Legislature in 1896. The intent of the law was twofold: to increase the excise tax on the sale of liquor and to cut down the number of dealers in liquor in the state of New York. To effect these two changes the law declared that in the licensing of an establishment which dispensed liquor to be consumed on the premises, there should be no distinction between the types of establishments, as there had been hitherto. Under the Raines Law, hotels, restaurants, public houses (bars in today's parlance), and ordinary beer saloons were charged the same price, a high one, for their licenses. The distinctions that were made were statewide and were made on the basis of population, that is, the higher the population of the city or town wherein the establishment was located, the higher the price of the license. Therefore the real tax increase fell on the proprietors in New York City, and the smallest proprietors there carried the heaviest burden. When in 1903, for example, seven years after the Raines Law was enacted, the taxes were increased once more, four hundred small beer saloons were wiped out. But small proprietors in Harry Hope's class, who dealt in spirits, suffered grievously too. George Washington Plunkitt was especially incensed by the Raines Law because it discriminated against the small and poorer saloonkeeper, as contrasted to the hotelkeeper. Plunkitt claimed to have known personally of a half-dozen small saloonkeepers who, unable to pay the enormous license fee and faced with the loss of their business, committed sui-

[6] See Joseph Rountree and Arthur Sherwell, *The Taxation of the Liquor Trade* (London, 1906), pp. 352 ff.

cide. He had heard of others: "Every time there is an increase of the fee,
there is an increase in the suicide record of the city" (Riordon, pp.
113-14). Whether this assertion is true cannot be proved, but certainly
the enactment of the Raines Law in 1896, and its further implemen-
tation in 1903, must have seriously contributed to the decay of Harry
Hope's saloon.

The Raines Law had two side effects that were not anticipated in
the original legislation and that play some role in *The Iceman Cometh*. There was written into the statute a Blue Law aimed expressly at
the saloons, to the effect that only hotels could serve liquor after
hours and on Sundays, the times at which the saloons did some of their
best business. Accordingly, every saloon that could manage to do so
immediately turned itself into a "hotel restaurant," by renting rooms
upstairs and by putting on the tables, in O'Neill's words, "a property
sandwich . . . an old desiccated ruin of dust-laden bread and mumified
ham or cheese." The most profitable thing to do with the rooms usually was to rent them out for sexual intercourse, the result being that
many of the saloons became, in effect, brothels (Werner, p. 405). Now
Harry Hope is still holding up his head in two respects: first, he still
has enough connections at the Hall to dispense with putting out the
property food on the tables (*"except during the fleeting alarms of
reform agitation"*), and, second, although he has tarts rooming at his
establishment, they do not carry on their trade there. As Harry says in
Act I, "Never thought I'd see the day when Harry Hope's would have
tarts rooming in it. What'd Bessie think? But I don't let 'em use my
rooms for business." Still, he and his kind have fallen on evil times,
and most of the New York characters in the play, while they lament
and glorify their individual mistakes and past, are also paying a collective obsequy to the "good old days," the 1890's, when giants walked
the earth, when corruption was direct, open, and simple, when "de
Chief," whoever he was, was tangible and approachable, and when
they were respectable "middle-class" (neither powers nor riffraff) members of the Tammany organization. The circus, and its ways, have
provided the same frame of memory for Mosher.

This collective nostalgia blends into the private nostalgia of each
character, New Yorker or not. It is, I think, an oversimplification
to say that all these characters are special cases of preoccupation with
the past because they are failures and down-and-outers; rather they
represent, each in his own way, the real vagaries of the human memory, which must both simplify and glorify, if ever so slightly in a
more happy and healthy climate than that of *The Iceman Cometh*,
the past. It is not that all men have been fired from their jobs as
drunks and thieves, as have some of the characters in *The Iceman*,
but all men have done things they would like to forget and they all

have at least some happy memories, which they would like to be even happier, and simpler, and to have bulked larger, in time and importance, than they actually had done in reality. It is by use of an artistically, artificially shaped past that man defends himself against the threatening present and the ominous future. A man is only genuinely lost when the past contains something mortal and deadly, like Hickey's murder of his wife and Parritt's betrayal of his mother. Almost anything else memory can take care of.

Music is, of course, the great evocator of memory, and especially in middle-class and lower-class America is popular music expressive of certain sentimental certainties that the memory would like to believe in and re-embrace, hastening back over the years to simpler and happier times and occasions. This is why popular songs play a role in *The Iceman Cometh* and even more of a role in *Ah, Wilderness!*

Popular songs gravitate between the bawdy and the sentimental; thus the two songs sung in *The Iceman Cometh* are Oban's "Sailor Lad" ditty (bawdy) and "She's the Sunshine of Paradise Alley" (sentimental). The choruses of songs dealt out to the various characters at the end, with Hickey gone, the "booze" working again, the present and future banished, were carefully chosen to perform two nostalgic functions: first, to awaken memories in the minds of the older people in the audience of the 1940's who saw the play performed for the first time and who, like the playwright, had memories of pre-World War I America, and, second, to invoke nostalgia in the minds of the characters in the play, whose memories extend back into the nineteenth century.

Although O'Neill chose his songs with extreme care for their historical date, he did commit one anachronism, a perfectly understandable one. This occurs in the musical medley at the end when Chuck is given "The Curse of an Aching Heart." Actually this song, by Henry Fink and Al Piantadesti, was not published until 1913 and could thus not have been known by people in 1912. However, the song itself was a purposeful anachronism and is made up of, in Sigmund Spaeth's phrase, "the maudlin absurdities" of the 1890's. Thus for the characters in the play it does invoke nostalgia. All the other songs sung at the end fall into one of two basic categories: either they are songs that were popular around 1912, or they are songs from the past.

"A Wee Dock and Doris," Jimmy Tomorrow's song, was published by Harry Lauder and Gerald Grafton in 1911; "Everybody's Doing It," appropriately given to Pearl and Margie, was published by Irving Berlin in 1911; "The Oceana Roll," Cora's, was done by Roger Lewis and Lucien Denni in 1911; and Rocky's "You Beautiful Doll" was perpetrated in 1911 by A. Seymour Brown and Nat Ayer. These songs, presumably, would be remembered by many of O'Neill's audience.

All the other songs, however, like "She's the Sunshine of Paradise
Alley," are nostalgia-invokers for the members of the cast. Wetjoen's
"Waiting at the Church" (also sung in *Ah, Wilderness!*) by Fred Leigh
and Henry E. Pether, was vintage 1906; Joe Mott's "All I Got Was
Sympathy" (actually the song was entitled "Sympathy"; O'Neill is
using the first line of the lyrics) was put together by Kendis and Pauley
in 1905; "Tammany," sung, appropriately, by McGloin, was an af-
fectionate but lively satire on Tammany politics concocted by Gus
Edwards and Vincent P. Bryan in 1905.

"Tammany" in particular, and the circumstances under which it
was written illustrate most concretely what Harry Hope, Joe Mott,
McGloin, and the rest mean by New York's "good old days," the time
when they were part of a political corruption which was not only
open, and cheerfully so, but had such a sense of humor about itself
as to make it almost endearing. According to a tradition run down
by Sigmund Spaeth, "Tammany" was composed under the following
circumstances (whether this story is true or not, it should be): Edwards
and Bryan were invited to entertain the members of New York's
Democratic Club at a smoker. They had planned to introduce their
new song, "In My Merry Oldsmobile," the best of many of the transportation songs of the day. But when they arrived at the smoker, the
orchestra was playing a medley of the Indian songs that were so popular at the time, and so they decided, on the spot, to compose a bur-
lesque of this type of music which would also be a political satire on
Tammany, whose name was Indian in origin. The two retired to a
room and worked out the chorus and two verses, with Edwards putting
down the notes as fast as Bryan could write the words. In the lyrics
there are references to *Hiawatha* and *Navaho,* all building up to
"Big Chief Tammany." They tried out this song first on a small
group of important Tammanyites, including Charlie Murphy and
"Big Tim" Sullivan. With their approval, Edwards and Bryan then
presented it to the whole group. It was a great and immediate success
and later became the official anthem of the Tammany Society (Spaeth,
pp. 347-48).

After these songs, however, we are back in the nineteenth century:
Ed Mosher's "Break the News to Mother," by Charles K. Harris, was
a Spanish-American War song, vintage 1897; Harry Hope's "She's the
Sunshine of Paradise Alley" (1895); Oban's "Sailor Lad" ditty (the sea)
is an immemorial folk song, as is Captain Lewis' "The Old Kent
Road" (the land); and, of course, with Hugo's "Carmagnole" we are
back to the French Revolution. As Hickey and Parritt go to their
deaths, all of the other happy sinners, Larry excepted, are sinking
gratefully back into nostalgia, alcoholic and tuneful.

Hugo of *The Iceman Cometh*:
Realism and O'Neill

by Doris M. Alexander

Because of its obvious semantic sloppiness, the term *realism* is used with caution by critics. Usually they find safety by implying or stating their definition of *realism* when they use it. Yet such is the treachery of the concept, that a critic may be betrayed by his own definition; a critic may sincerely damn as unrealistic a work that fulfills in all respects his own definition of *realism*. Trapped in this way, by his own terminology, is the critic who describes Hugo Kalmar of *The Iceman Cometh* as "unrealistic," "literary."

In his "Trying to Like O'Neill," Eric Bentley finds the chief weakness of *The Iceman Cometh,* and of most later O'Neill plays, in the author's "ambition to transcend realism." According to Bentley, O'Neill "was a good playwright insofar as he kept within the somewhat narrow range of his own sensibility." O'Neill is artistically safe "when he stays close to a fairly simple reality and when, by way of technique, he uses fairly simple forms of realism." But when he tries to express ideas, O'Neill is, according to Bentley, lost. "He is so little a thinker, it is dangerous for him to think." This thesis, Bentley applies to *The Iceman Cometh,* finding in the play "a genuine and a non-genuine element, the former, which we regarded as the core, being realistic, the latter, which we took as inessential excrescence, being expressionistic." For this reason, Bentley finds it necessary "to cut away the rotten fruit of unreality" around the play. The one concrete instance he gives of this "rotten fruit" is the characterization of Hugo:

> One can cut down the speeches of Hugo since they are both too long and too pretentious. It is such a pretentiousness, replete with obvious and unimaginative symbolism, that constitutes the expressionism of the play. Hugo is a literary conception—by Gorky out of Dostoevsky.[1]

"Hugo of The Iceman Cometh: *Realism and O'Neill," by Doris M. Alexander. From* American Quarterly, *V (Winter, 1953), 357-66. Copyright © 1953 by American Quarterly. Reprinted by permission of the author and publisher.*

[1] Eric Bentley, "Trying to Like O'Neill," *Kenyon Review*, XIV, Summer 1952, pp. 476-92, and pp. 483, 488, 491, 478, 479.

When Bentley damns Hugo categorically as "a literary conception," he has either forgotten, never known, or never believed O'Neill's own statement that all the characters of *The Iceman Cometh* are people he knew personally. In the *New York Times,* October 6, 1946, Karl Schriftgriesser reported O'Neill's comment during an interview on the characters of *The Iceman Cometh*:

> "I knew 'em all," he said. "I've known 'em all for years." His voice dropped gropingly into his remembrance of things past. "All these people I have written about, I once knew."

Critics who attacked the play at the time of its Broadway production could not forget O'Neill's statement, and so they had to attack O'Neill, not for trying to "transcend realism," but rather for being unable to give an accurate representation of the reality he was offering. Take, for example, Wolcott Gibbs' criticism of *The Iceman Cometh* in the October 19, 1946, issue of the *New Yorker*:

> As several critics have pointed out, the locale of the play and the proto-types of the bums who appear in it have been taken from the author's own past. The assumption, however, that he has exactly recaptured the sound of their speech may be open to question, and it is my opinion that, while Mr. O'Neill is a superb reporter of behavior and even of processes of thought, the language he uses to convey them is actually non-realistic, being of the conventional dese-dem-dose school of dialect which a certain kind of abstracted literary intelligence, from Richard Harding Davis to Thomas Wolfe, has somewhat arbitrarily decided is the language of the lower depths. It is odd but nevertheless a fact that a writer can often understand perfectly what is being said around him without really hearing the accent of the voice or the structure of the sentence, and I'm afraid that this is particularly true of Mr. O'Neill.[2]

Of course, this criticism is aimed at all the characters, not specifically at Hugo, but that Gibbs finds Hugo particularly unconvincing appears earlier in his article where he points out that in Hugo's characterization "all that appears on the stage is a sort of irrelevant, comic-supplement bomb-thrower."[3]

In order to test the accuracy of Bentley's idea that Hugo is totally a "literary conception" or Gibbs' idea that though Hugo derives ulti-mately from life he has been distorted by an "abstracted literary intel-ligence," we would have to know definitely first whether Hugo was modeled on a living person, and second, what that living person was actually like. Fortunately, we can establish these facts with a fair amount of certainty. O'Neill's own statement that he knew all of the characters in *The Iceman Cometh* gives us our clue. If so colorful a

---

[2] Wolcott Gibbs, "The Theatre," *New Yorker* (October 19, 1946), pp. 56-57.
[3] *Ibid.,* p. 56.

character as Hugo actually existed in a literary circle like the one
at Provincetown, he might appear in the memoirs of one of the group.
This is exactly the case. In Mabel Dodge Luhan's *Movers and Shakers*
and in Hutchins Hapgood's *A Victorian in the Modern World* are
references to an extraordinary gentleman who appears to be, without
a doubt, the model for O'Neill's Hugo in *The Iceman Cometh*.

Among the Provincetown group was an anarchist named Hippolyte
Havel. Mabel Dodge Luhan describes him as "a Russian nihilist with
a broad, low, intelligent brow, and long, black hair; he was very
small, and very obscene in his talk." [4] This definition resembles, as
far as it goes, O'Neill's description of Hugo Kalmar.

> Hugo is a small man in his late fifties. He has a head much too big for
> his body, a high forehead, crinkly long black hair streaked with gray,
> a square face with a pug nose, a walrus mustache, black eyes which
> peer near-sightedly from behind thick-lensed spectacles, tiny hands and
> feet. . . . There is a foreign atmosphere about him, the stamp of an
> alien radical, a strong resemblance to the type Anarchist as portrayed,
> bomb in hand, in newspaper cartoons.[5]

This description fits Mabel Dodge Luhan's, but there are not enough
points of resemblance to make an absolute identification. We do not
have to rely on Mabel Dodge Luhan's meager description alone, however, for in Hutchins Hapgood's *A Victorian in the Modern World*
at one side of a photograph labeled "Group in Provincetown about
1916" sits Hippolyte Havel himself, and so we can compare both
O'Neill's description and Mabel Dodge Luhan's with a photographic
likeness of the original. From the picture it becomes clear at once
that O'Neill's description of Hugo Kalmar is a better sketch of Hippolyte Havel than is Mabel Dodge Luhan's description of Havel himself. In the photograph Hippolyte's long black hair appears "crinkly,"
for it stands out around his head like a halo, and it is clearly streaked
with gray, a detail that Mabel Dodge Luhan does not include in her
description.[6] Also Mrs. Luhan's description of his "broad, low, intelligent brow" is actually, although accurate, misleading, for a "low
brow" is usually associated with a low forehead, whereas the picture
of Hippolyte Havel shows a positively astonishing height and breadth
of forehead, so that the face appears to be pinched together at the

[4] Mabel Dodge Luhan, *Movers and Shakers*, vol. 3 of *Intimate Memories* (New
York: Harcourt, Brace, 1936), p. 48. Hutchins Hapgood, who knew Hippolyte Havel
better, reports: "One of Hippolyte's parents was a gypsy; and I think most of his
blood was of that part of Austria called Bohemia. . . ." Hutchins Hapgood, *A
Victorian in the Modern World* (New York: Harcourt, Brace, 1939), p. 198.

[5] Eugene O'Neill, *The Iceman Cometh* (New York: Random House, 1946), p. 4.

[6] Possibly Havel's hair was not as noticeably gray in 1913, when Mabel Dodge
Luhan knew him, as in 1916.

bottom. The picture also confirms O'Neill's details of the square face, the pug nose, the walrus mustache, and the spectacles, which, in the photograph, are horn rimmed and very prominent.[7] The only aspect of O'Neill's description not borne out by the picture is his account of Hugo's clothing: "He is dressed in threadbare black clothes and his white shirt is frayed at collar and cuffs, but everything about him is fastidiously clean. Even his flowing Windsor tie is neatly tied." [8] We might believe that here at least O'Neill is exaggerating his original, were it not for Hapgood's description of Havel's customary attire for a weekend in Greenwich Village: "a stick, conventional black clothes, a flowing black tie, and even spats with his patent leather shoes." [9] Altogether, there are too many similarities between Hugo Kalmar and Hippolyte Havel for their resemblance to be merely a coincidence.

Nor are these similarities limited to appearance. The central facts of Hugo's life exactly parallel the main points of Hippolyte Havel's. First, in order to qualify as a member of Harry Hope's menage, Hugo is, of course, both impecunious and alcoholic. So was his original Hippolyte Havel. According to Hapgood: "Hippolyte was a determined drinker. To drink much and often was a part of his code of honor. It was limited only by his pocketbook which was usually empty, and the fact that although he had many friends, he couldn't always count on their treating him." [10] Hugo, like Hippolyte, depends on the benevolence of his friends, and O'Neill makes one of the staples of his conversation the remark: "Don't be a fool! Loan me a dollar! Buy me a trink!" [11] Apparently, even the amount of Hugo's request is patterned after his original, for Hapgood points out that Hippolyte frequently "would ask me for a dollar," and tells how once when he met Hippolyte on a Fifth Avenue bus, "he characteristically asked me for a dollar, which I dutifully handed over to him." [12] Even the more spectacular facts of Hugo's background are identical with Hippolyte's. O'Neill describes Hugo as a "one-time editor of Anarchist periodicals." [13] Hapgood tells how, when they met, Havel "was the editor of the *Arbeiterzeitung*, an Anarchist newspaper in Chicago." [14] More-

---

[7] O'Neill's description is also substantiated by Hutchins Hapgood's description of Havel: "He was a short, rather stocky, excitable man, with a very small nose, accentuating a high and imaginative forehead, a rather weak and sensitive chin—with a shock of black disorderly hair crowning the whole. He was in a perpetual state of vituperative excitement." Hapgood, p. 198.

[8] O'Neill, p. 4.

[9] Hapgood, p. 328.

[10] *Ibid.*

[11] O'Neill, p. 34. See also pp. 11, 104, 249.

[12] Hapgood, p. 330.

[13] O'Neill, p. v.

[14] Hapgood, p. 198.

over, even Hugo's prison experience accords with Hippolyte's. In *The Iceman Cometh* we learn from Parritt that Hugo "had the guts to serve ten years in the can in his own country and get his eyes ruined in solitary." [15] Hapgood's description of Hippolyte Havel's background is similar, although far more colorful:

> Before coming to America, Hippolyte had been sentenced to prison in an insane asylum; and, as he put it, might have been there permanently, as in that way his sentence could be indefinitely prolonged, had it not been for the visit of Krafft-Ebing, the noted psychiatrist, to the institution. After a talk with Hippolyte, Krafft-Ebing told the authorities that Hippolyte should be sent back to prison, as he was entirely sane. The great psychiatrist showed himself superior to the ordinary citizens, who, judging from Hippolyte's words and manner, might be excused for thinking him somewhere unbalanced. But anyone who knew him well, would know that he was not only sane, but much shrewder in practical things than he would ever admit. In some way he managed to escape from prison and got safe to London, where he met Emma Goldman, and with her or through her came to America and was associated with her for many years in her journalistic and oratorical propaganda.[16]

Hugo Kalmar, like his prototype Hippolyte Havel, has been an Anarchist editor, has been imprisoned in his own country, and, finally, has been and is "a determined drinker."

O'Neill has certainly been accurate in reproducing Havel's physical appearance and the main outlines of his life. But how are we to judge his accuracy in reproducing Havel's personality? Hutchins Hapgood gives us the outstanding features of Havel's personality in the following account:

> Then another character of the village whom Christine rendered with felicity was Hippolyte Havel, the wild little man about whom I have had much to say, who was always strenuously inveighing against the damn bourgeois. Although he was dark and Christine was blonde, yet, when Christine was imitating Hippolyte, the portrait was so good that Christine almost looked dark. This portrait must have been extraordinarily good because I couldn't detect any satire in it. It didn't seem to convey a criticism, perhaps because Hippolyte himself conveyed his own criticism by his actual appearance on the scene of life. This remark of mine about Hippolyte would be entirely inadequate were it not for what I have already written or shall write about him. Mean, vindictive, or jealous as Hippolyte often was, and irrationally condemnatory of almost all the world, there was in him something exquisitely sensitive, fine, and at times highly amusing in a sympathetic sense.[17]

[15] O'Neill, p. 34.
[16] Hapgood, p. 199.
[17] Hapgood, p. 426.

This description of a "wild little man" who inveighs against the
"damn bourgeois" and "all the world" for that matter, who alternates
between meanness, vindictiveness, and being highly amusing, seems
a pretty close description of O'Neill's little anarchist, Hugo Kalmar,
of *The Iceman Cometh*. Hugo's first speech reveals the essentials of
his character and conversation.

> (*Raises his head and peers at* ROCKY *blearily through his thick specta-
> cles—in a guttural declamatory tone*) Capitalist swine! Bourgeois stool
> pigeons! Have the slaves no right to sleep even? (*Then he grins at*
> ROCKY *and his manner changes to a giggling, wheedling playfulness,
> as though he were talking to a child*) Hello, leedle Rocky! Leedle
> monkey face! Vere is your leedle slave girls? (*With an abrupt change
> to a bullying tone*) Don't be a fool! Loan me a dollar! Damned bour-
> geois Wop! The great Malatesta is my good friend! Buy me a trink! [18]

Of course, there is no indication in this speech of what Hapgood re-
fers to as "something exquisitely sensitive, fine" in Havel. But in later
speeches of Hugo, O'Neill presents some sensitivity in his character,
particularly in Hugo's comment on Harry deprived of his pipe dream.
"Vhat's matter, Harry? You look funny. You look dead. Vhat's happened?" [19]

However, even if we have demonstrated that O'Neill conveyed accurately the substance of Havel's conversation, there is still the possibility that Gibbs is correct, and O'Neill has been unable to catch
"the accent of the voice or the structure of the sentence." But even
this can be checked, for Mabel Dodge Luhan has given us a specimen
of Hippolyte Havel's actual conversation, which shows, by the way,
how universal was his condemnation of the world as "bourgeois." She
reports Havel's reactions to a conversation by Emma Goldman and
Big Bill Haywood on the philosophy of the Industrial Workers of
the World, and of socialism.

> "They talk like goddam bourgeois," suddenly cried Hippolyte Havel
> in a high, peevish voice, glaring around through the thick lenses of his
> spectacles.
> "My little sister!" he exclaimed to me later that evening, in his sweet
> whining voice. "My little goddam bourgeois capitalist sister!" And tears
> ran over his spectacles.[20]

Except that O'Neill is careful to represent Havel's accent, and Mabel
Dodge Luhan does not attempt to, this actual specimen of Hippolyte
Havel's conversation might be inserted as part of Hugo Kalmar's dia-
logue in *The Iceman Cometh* without any alteration but the name

[18] O'Neill, p. 11.
[19] O'Neill, p. 201.
[20] Luhan, p. 90.

of the speaker. Unless we assume that Mabel Dodge Luhan was suffering from the same kind of literary astigmatism as was Eugene O'Neill, and hence both have missed the flavor of Hippolyte Havel's speech, we reach the inevitable conclusion that O'Neill has done a very accurate job of reporting the flavor, the style, of his original. Altogether, it is difficult to escape the conclusion that in the character of Hugo Kalmar, Eugene O'Neill has reproduced most accurately in literature a character he knew in life.[21]

What then of Eric Bentley's and Wolcott Gibbs' condemnation of Hugo as "literary," the product of an "abstracted literary intelligence"? First, what is their definition of the realism they think Hugo lacks? Bentley's definition can be gathered only by implication, but from his statement that O'Neill "was a good playwright insofar as he kept within the somewhat narrow range of his own sensibility," Bentley's realism seems to consist of a fairly photographic reproduction of life. When describing his stage set for the Berlin production of *The Iceman Cometh,* Bentley says, "we tried simply to underline the sheer reality, the sheer banality and ugliness, of its locale." Here banality and ugliness stand in apposition to reality, again suggesting a photographic approach. Later Bentley points out that he didn't go "to the other extreme—a piddling and illusion-mongering naturalism." Also, when he analyzes O'Neill's note on Strindberg, Bentley comments: "So far, so good. This is only a warning against that extreme and narrow form of realism generally known as naturalism. Everyone agrees. The mistake is only to talk as if it followed that one must get away from realism altogether. . . ." [22] Bentley seems to make a quantitative distinction between realism and naturalism, with naturalism simply including more details in its photograph. Whatever he holds realism to be, Bentley thinks it is endangered by philosophy, by selection on the basis of ideas. So it seems to be a fairly literal kind of reproduction of life. Gibbs' concept of realism seems very similar, since he defines the non-realism of O'Neill's dialogue as a failure to hear "the accent of the voice or the structure of the sentence" of the people he is reproducing in literature. So both critics base their idea of realism on a close reproduction of life, and then proceed to damn as unrealistic a character who has been modeled with the utmost exactitude on a living person.

What is wrong: the critics, their terminology, or their understanding of their terminology? Perhaps the difficulty lies in the use of an

---

[21] It is impossible that O'Neill did not know Havel, for they were at the same place, Provincetown, at the same time, with the same friends. For instance, Hapgood met Terry Carlin, O'Neill's lifelong friend, at the anarchist ball at which he met Hippolyte Havel. Hapgood, pp. 198-99. Harry Weinberger, who appears in the Provincetown photograph with Havel, was O'Neill's lawyer and friend for many years.

[22] Bentley, p. 484.

inexact concept as an instrument of criticism. Certainly Bentley and
Gibbs cannot be blamed for finding Hugo Kalmar somewhat fantastic, just as they couldn't be blamed for finding his prototype Hippolyte Havel somewhat fantastic if they happened to meet him. The
fault is not in the judgment, but in the theory of causation. Hugo
Kalmar is fantastic not because O'Neill, bedeviled by ideas, was unable to reproduce life, but rather because O'Neill chose to reproduce
a variety of life that is inherently grotesque. What Bentley is really
objecting to in Hugo is not his lack of closeness to life, but rather
his lack of closeness to typical life. As Hutchins Hapgood observed,
Christine could not satirize Hippolyte Havel "because Hippolyte
Havel conveyed his own criticism by his actual appearance on the
scene of life." In other words, Havel's eccentricities could not be exaggerated into satire, for they were already so exaggerated that he
was a living satire. Hippolyte Havel was neither a typical human
being nor a typical anarchist. A literary reproduction of him, were
it ever so accurate, could not be more than he was himself, an eccen-
tric, a caricature. O'Neill's representation is certainly accurate. Thus
only if we assume that realism is reproduction of the typical, can we
attack Hugo for lacking it.

Why did O'Neill choose to reproduce an atypical character like
Hippolyte Havel? Undoubtedly the same principle operated in the
selection of Hippolyte Havel as operated in the selection of all the
other characters in *The Iceman Cometh*, for all the characters are
variations on a single theme. All the characters are illustrative of a
single principle. Each must cling to a pipe dream, to a patently false
illusion, to keep from facing his own hopeless inadequacy and his
submerged hostilities toward his fellow men.[23] Which came first for
O'Neill, the principle or the characters? Karl Schriftgriesser, in his
New York Times interview with O'Neill, reported that the idea for
The Iceman Cometh came suddenly to O'Neill and that because he
knew all the characters so well, there "was not so much hard work
as if I had had to dig them out." From this statement I infer that
O'Neill's idea for *The Iceman Cometh* came from thinking of the
people like Hippolyte Havel he had known, and hence, once he had
the idea for the play, he had the characters too. Most likely O'Neill
did not alter the characters to conform to the idea, but rather saw
the idea in the characters as they were. For instance, the character
of Jimmy Tomorrow, complete with his illusion, had already appeared
in one of O'Neill's earliest plays *The Moon of the Caribbees*. In that
play he appears as the sentimental Smitty. Both as Jimmy Tomorrow

---

[23] For a full and very fine analysis of *The Iceman Cometh's* ideology, see Helen
Muchnic, "Circe's Swine: Plays by Gorky and O'Neill," *Comp. Lit.*, III (Spring
1951), pp. 119-28.

and as Smitty, his pipe dream consists of the illusion that he is an alcoholic because the woman he loved left him. In *The Moon of the Caribbees*, Smitty's illusion is exposed by the Donkeyman: "An' she said she threw you over 'cause you was drunk; an' you said you was drunk 'cause she threw you over." [24] In *The Iceman Cometh*, Jimmy Tomorrow, under the influence of Hickey, confesses: "And it was absurd of me to excuse my drunkenness by pretending it was my wife's adultery that ruined my life. As Hickey guessed, I was a drunkard before that. Long before." [25] Smitty needed no basic alteration to become Jimmy Tomorrow of *The Iceman Cometh*, and most likely all of the characters of *The Iceman Cometh* were as naturally illustrative of the idea of the play.

If it is correct to assume that all the characters of *The Iceman Cometh*, like Hippolyte Havel, are faithful reproductions of actual people who by their very nature are illustrative of the idea of the play, what conclusions may be drawn on the value of the play itself? First, perhaps the greatest value of the play lies in all the, to use Hugo's expression, "nice, leedle, funny monkey faces" in it. O'Neill told Barrett Clark that *The Iceman Cometh* is one of the two plays that have given him the greatest satisfaction of any he has ever done.[26] Probably his satisfaction lay in the vivid re-creation of a group of broken, but strangely lovable, people he had known. In the characters also lies, perhaps, the satisfaction of any who read or see the play. Whatever enduring value *The Iceman Cometh* holds consists, probably, not in its dramatic or ideological qualities, but in its fine character sketches of a group of fascinating lost souls.

[24] Eugene O'Neill, *The Plays of Eugene O'Neill*, 3 vols. (New York: Random House, 1941), I, 467.
[25] O'Neill, *The Iceman Cometh*, p. 229.
[26] Barrett H. Clark, *Eugene O'Neill: The Man and His Plays* (New York: Dover, 1947), p. 147.

The Iceman Cometh: A Study in Technique

by Sophus Winther

O'Neill's latest play *The Iceman Cometh*, is his most symbolic, although it uses none of the direct symbolism of such plays as the *Great God Brown* and *Lazarus Laughed*. Anyone familiar with O'Neill's work in its entirety will recall the intricate way in which life and death, hope and fear, the dream and the reality are woven into the core of each central theme. In no other play are these symbols brought so closely together or so perfectly conceived as in *The Iceman Cometh*. In the words of Larry, one of the characters in *The Iceman Cometh*, the "worst is best here, and East is West, and tomorrow is yesterday." Later Larry gives a more comprehensive statement of the extent to which life's paradoxes are reduced to unity with all conflicts reconciled into complete nothingness.

> Honor or dishonor, faith or treachery are nothing to me but the opposites of the same stupidity which is ruler and king of life, and in the end they rot into dust in the same grave. All things are the same meaningless joke to me, for they grin at me from the one skull of death.

The recognition of the paradox[1] treated not as a clever device for satire, but as a serious instrument of tragedy is the key to the art as well as to the meaning of the play. In no other play has O'Neill combined his technical skill so completely with a searching analysis of life. No separation of thought from technique will reveal the meaning of the play. The paradox reigns supreme: the dream is the true reality, reality is a dream, hope leads to despair, despair breeds hope; the Cause, Movement, Crusade, all lead to Harry Hope's hotel, "a cheap ginmill" of the "last resort variety." The paradox brings that close juxtaposition of opposites which in time reduces all opposites to a oneness. The problem is to define clearly all operating forces in the tragedy, to identify them as irreconcilable opposites and then,

---

"The Iceman Cometh: *A Study in Technique*," by *Sophus Winther. From* Arizona Quarterly, *III* (*Winter, 1947*), *293-300. Copyright* © *1946 by* Arizona Quarterly. *Reprinted by permission of the author and publisher.*

[1] See Cleanth Brooks on paradox, *The Well Wrought Urn.*

through the introduction of the proper catalyst, slowly melt them into one.

This is the common practice in great tragedy. It must test man not in the middle course of life, nor by the ordinary burdens that are a part of everyday experience. Tragedy must push man to the verge of his ultimate endurance until he stands on the bank and shoal of time, until he cries out "Let us anatomize Regan to see if there be any cause in nature that makes these hard hearts." The quality of man, like the tensile strength of steel, is measured at the breaking point. The outward contradictions provide the action which leads to the reconciliation of the paradox, an inward unity which is the tragic end.

O'Neill brings before his readers a group of characters who at the first casual glance have lost every shred of humanity. They seem to have passed the breaking point, to have reached the place of slow but inevitable decay. O'Neill compares them to dogs, turkeys, horses, monkeys; they are remnants of men, scarecrows who have in some strange manner cheated the undertaker. For them there is nothing left except pipe dreams nourished and kept alive by rotgut whisky. Before the slightest breath of the outside world they tremble and shake like an old dog in his sleep. They are utterly broken. They are dead shadows of human beings, but the paradox is that they are all this, while at the same time they are symbols of all that is meaningful in the life of man. There are among them some whose history is not revealed fully. The reason for the pimps and whores is not explained. Perhaps they need no explanation, being the normal product of a world that has brought Oban, Larry, Jimmy Tomorrow, Hugo, and Harry Hope to the brink of the ultimate Slough of Despond.

Each in his own way was destroyed by his faith in the Cause, The Big Movement, the Ideal of what man should be. Willie Oban has made his final visit to the hockshop. His few pieces of clothing look as though they were made "of an inferior grade of dirty blotting paper." His bare feet show through his ragged shoes. His face continually twitches, his eyelids blink as though the light were too strong for them. Larry is a disinterested observer. He has taken "a seat in the grandstand of philosophic detachment" from which he expects to fall asleep "observing the cannibals do their death dance." His favorite quotation is from Heine:

> Lo, sleep is good, better is death; in sooth
> The best of all were never to be born.

Hugo is neat and clean, but in some ways the most utterly desolate of them all. His one desire is enough booze to keep him asleep, his one theme, "The days grow hot, O Babylon! 'Tis cool beneath thy willow trees!"

Harry Hope, owner of the hotel which provides the setting, has not left the place for twenty years. He would seem to be the most useless of men, the most completely detached from anything that is meaningful to the normal world of men.

And so are they all upon first sight, as useless, degenerate, and physically and morally ragged as human beings could possibly be. They hang on the shadowy threads of life like spiders clinging to a hopelessly ruined and tangled web. They are sustained by a poisonous brew that should have turned them over to the undertaker long ago. But the paradox is that they are also symbols of the ideals by which men live. They have fought in the Cause. They have been leaders of the Great Movement. They were heroes in wars, national and social. Hugo served ten years in prison for the Cause. Each in his own way has been apprenticed to the Ideal, and when the Ideal failed he drifted to this Last Resort Saloon where he nourishes his pipe dream and drinks rotgut whisky, waiting for the Big Day. Each in his own way is the complete paradox. Each reveals both sides of the badly minted coin at a single glance. They are the contradiction which is man.

Larry has seen that greed is stronger than any other power in man, that man will "never pay the price of liberty." The whole show is for him a meaningless joke. Hugo has discovered that the proletariat are swine, Oban that his father was a traitor to his son and to the ideals of the state. Harry Hope is constantly defeated and tortured by his loyalty to his friends and the realization of their utterly futile lives.

Each in his turn has developed a pipe dream by which he clings to such shreds of self-respect as are necessary to life. All wait for the turning of the "new leaf" for the "Tomorrow" that never comes, for the ship "loaded to the gunwales with cancelled regrets and promises fulfilled and clean slates and new leases." The "Favoring breeze has the stink of nickel whiskey on its breath. Truth is irrelevant and immaterial. To hell with truth." The whole "misbegotten mad lot" of them is long overdue for the loaded shroud and the green quiet of the bottom of the sea. For them the crows have already made wing to the rocky wood. Night's black angels are approaching for the ultimate feast. Yet they are the symbol of man's humanity.

As the characters are symbols, emphasized and made convincing by the paradox of being outcasts of the lowest order, who under their rags embody the only hope man has in an ideal world, so the place in which they live is made symbolical by the paradox. It is a "morgue wid all de stiffs on deck." The morgue theme is carried throughout the play. The morgue is man's shelter, a place where he is dead or dying or just waiting for death; it is man's world. It is a place from which Harry Hope imagines his dead wife doing "somersaults in her grave" while his companions shake and tremble with "the graveyard fantods." It is the "morgue on a rainy Sunday night," and it is also the "Palace of Pipe Dreams," the shelter where man's last hope for salvation is preserved in cheap whisky. Beneath its filthy exterior, its apparent degradation, lies its complete opposite, the gentle warmth of a home and the tender kindness of Harry Hope.

Into this paradoxical little corner of the world comes the catalytic agent, Hickey, the Iceman of Death, the symbol of salvation, the greatest paradox of all. Into the "Calm atmosphere" of the "Last Harbor," this place as "harmless as a graveyard," where man lives by "the consolation that he hasn't far to go," comes Hickey. This salesman, whose father was a preacher in Indiana, a man of God who sold "Hoosier hayseeds building lots along the Golden Street!" is on first appearance a cheap drummer. He is known for his drinking and carousing, and most of all for his stories, which include lewd references to his wife, Evelyn, and the iceman who consoles her while Hickey is away from home. O'Neill makes him the epitome of the commonplace in order that the paradox which is the essence of tragedy may be the more startling and effective.

Slowly and ingeniously, the opposite Hickey is revealed. The first indication is the remark, "Would Hickey or Death would come." This is emphasized by Hugo's theme of Babylon, and the growing realization that the iceman about whom Hickey has joked is "The Iceman of Death . . . Death was the Iceman Hickey called to his home." This no-account, irresponsible drummer takes on strange forms. The inhabitants of The Last Resort begin to realize that their place, a symbol of man's world, is the antechamber to the morgue, that Larry, the Barker for the Big Sleep, has spoken more truly than he knew.

An ominous atmosphere develops around Hickey as an emissary of Death. Larry says, "I'm damned sure he brought death with him. I could feel the cold touch of him." And later he reaffirms his feeling, "Didn't I tell you he brought death with him?" There is about Hickey "Something not human behind his damned grinning and kidding." Hickey recognizes this feeling and tries to dispel it by saying, "We don't want corpses at this feast." This is a conscious emphasis on the paradox which is the dramatist's problem, for he realizes what the reader only suspects vaguely, that Hickey the Salesman must become the Saviour.

Gradually Hickey's mission becomes clear. He has appeared in a new guise. He has come to save men from their illusions, their pipe dreams. Larry recognizes it first, because he has achieved a semblance of philosophic detachment. He tells his comrades that Hickey has the "miraculous touch to raise the dead." It should have been apparent earlier because as the ending of the first act approaches, Hickey feels the strange power of his message come over him and he urges his potential disciples to, "Let yourself sink down to the bottom of the sea. Rest in peace. There is no further you have to go. Not a single damned hope or dream left to nag you."

Finally his true character appears. Like Jesus he has mystical insight and understanding. He tells Parritt that he knows everything. "You can't hide yourself, not even here on the bottom of the sea." And later to all of them he says, "I know every one of you inside out by heart." Hickey, like the Saviour, recognizes that his time is short.

> I saw I couldn't do what I was after alone. Not in the time at my disposal. I knew when I came here I wouldn't be able to stay with you long. I'm slated to leave on a trip. I saw I'd have to hustle and use every means I could.

His consciousness of being on his Father's business grows upon him, and with it comes that divine certainty which only the God-inspired can have.

> I swear I'd never act like I have if I wasn't absolutely sure it will be worth it to you in the end, after you're rid of the damned guilt . . . and the remorse that nags at you and makes you hide behind lousy pipe dreams about tomorrow. You'll be in a today where there is no yesterday or tomorrow to worry you.

The Scriptural echoes are too familiar to be missed, as is his new term of address "Brothers and Sisters." He will lead them where "no pipe dreams can ever nag at them again."

Before this great affirmation Hickey had told them "You won't be scared of either life or death any more." And Larry had foreseen the end and described it in his account of Harry Hope's birthday party as the "Second feast of Belshazzar with Hickey to do the writing on the wall." He had issued the warning, "Make sure first it's the real McCoy and not poison," a warning that coils around the central theme of all the Saviours who ever came to relieve the self-torture of mankind.

As the play approaches the end the paradox fades. Hickey is no longer a cheap drummer. His mystical qualities are felt in the lives of all the characters. Larry becomes entirely sincere in his deep hatred of "The stupid greed of the human circus." He is weighed down with the ironical pretense of human existence, "The dirty, stinking bit of withered flesh which is my beautiful little life." When Harry Hope comes back from the trial of faith, he feels "all in, like a corpse" and he appears to the others in the same light. He is like Lazarus when he came back from the grave. Hugo notices that Harry looks "Funny. You look dead," and Rocky adds, "He does look like he'd croaked," and Larry recognizes, "It's the peace of death you've brought him."

As the "peace" spreads it works like an active poison in the lives of all the characters. Hugo finds his subconscious speaking out, calling his beloved proletarians "Slaves," and life a crazy monkey face. "Always there is blood beneath the willow trees."

The Saviour who develops must not be construed literally as Jesus. He is just the Saviour, Christ, Buddha, perhaps most of all Lao Tze, for O'Neill has for many years been steeped in the philosophy of the religions of the East. In this play the Saviour is not the Messiah of a particular group but the Saviour of mankind. He embodies the Universal Saviour whose essence is Nihilism. Larry affirms this, telling the others that:

> It's not Bakunin's ghost you ought to pray to in your dreams, but to the great Nihilist, Hickey. He's started a movement that will blow up the world.

What Hickey preaches is the end of all dreams, all the pipe dreams, the end of all "Desire to communicate with the world . . . or . . . to be bothered with its greedy madness." It is the Buddhist's Nirvana, the Christian Heaven, but perhaps most of all the quietism of Lao Tze. It is the peace that comes when man no longer stirs the muddy pool but sits by its edge quietly until the roiled water grows still, the muddy particles settle, and finally the sun goes down, the stars fill the heavens and man is alone, quiet and at peace; beyond desire, pipe dreams, vague hopes and most of all, beyond the futility of actions.

Then, as the end of the play approaches, Hickey must fail, as all Saviours have failed. His magic does not work, his disciples are not happy. They are free from their pipe dreams, but life has lost its savor.

> By rights you should be contented by now, without a single damned hope or lying dream left to torment you! But here you are like a lot of stiffs cheating the undertaker . . . Can't you see there is no tomorrow now?

They are human. They can't live without their ideals and by their ideals they are doomed to torture themselves and each other today, tomorrow and forever as they have throughout their whole miserable and fantastic history. And as Hickey realizes his failure, he welcomes his doom. And the torture returns as his subconscious speaks out his hatred for Evelyn. He had called her a "Damned bitch," and now he must cry out for mercy in his last agony. Death will be the only end to his pipe dream. Larry expresses it, "May the Chair bring him peace at last, the poor tortured bastard."

The curtain falls as the paradox becomes complete. The "saved" actors return to their pipe dreams as men must, as they always have, acting out their part in the antechamber to the morgue. "The days grow hot, O Babylon!" There will be blood beneath the willow trees.

The Iceman and the Bridegroom: Some Observations on the Death of O'Neill's Salesman

by Cyrus Day

> While the bridegroom tarried, they all slumbered and slept. And at midnight there was a cry made, Behold, the bridegroom cometh.
>
> —Matthew 25:5-6

The Iceman Cometh is a play about the death of a salesman; its central theme is the relationship between men's illusions and their will to live. The salesman, Theodore Hickman, or Hickey, as he is called, is a more complex character than Arthur Miller's Willie Loman, and O'Neill's diagnosis of the spiritual *malaise* of the twentieth century is more profound than Miller's. Loman is depicted from the outside: he is the victim of a false and wholly external conception of what constitutes success. He wants, in a worldly sense, to solve the riddle of life, but the questions he asks are superficial and relatively easy for an audience or a reader to answer.

Hickey is depicted from the inside. He is more successful as a salesman than Loman, but he is the victim of a far more insidious disease. He is not versed at first hand (as O'Neill was) in philosophic nihilism, but he has somehow become aware, presumably through a sort of intellectual osmosis, that modern man no longer believes in objective reality and truth. Loman is adrift in contemporary American society; Hickey is adrift in the universe. The difference is a measure of the difference between O'Neill's aims and the aims of almost all other modern dramatists.

A few days before *The Iceman Cometh* opened on Broadway in 1946, O'Neill told a reporter that he had tried to express its "deeper" meaning in its title, and in an interview with S. J. Woolf he said that

"*The Iceman and the Bridegroom: Some Observations on the Death of O'Neill's Salesman*," by Cyrus Day. From **Modern Drama**, *I (May, 1958), 3-9. Copyright © 1958 by* Modern Drama. *Reprinted by permission of the publisher.*

the verb form "cometh" was a "deliberate reference to biblical language." The play itself, he gave Woolf to understand, had religious significance. It is difficult to see what he can have meant by these hints, for *The Iceman Cometh* has few readily discernible connections either with religion or with the Bible. However, since O'Neill was not in the habit of talking at random about his own work, we would do well, if we want to come to terms with the "deeper" meaning of *The Iceman Cometh,* to assume that he had something specific and important in mind, and to try to discover what it was.

O'Neill looked upon himself, we must remember, as a spiritual physician, and he thought that his mission as a dramatist was to "dig at the roots of the sickness of today," which he defined as the death of the old God (echoing Nietzsche) and the failure of science and materialism to provide a new one satisfactory to the remnants of man's primitive religious instincts. Most dramatists write about the relationship between man and man, but he was more interested, he said, in the relationship between man and God. His plays, accordingly, often have a metaphysical basis, but since he had lost his faith in God at an early period in his life, and since he thought that it would take a million years of evolution for man "to grow up and obtain a soul," they are seldom religious in any generally accepted sense of the word.

Days without End, which preceded *The Iceman Cometh,* is an exception. Written in 1934, during a brief period of personal happiness, it is a Christian play. The protagonist, a young man very much like O'Neill himself, is torn by religious doubts, but in the final act he enters a Catholic church, prostrates himself before an image of the crucified Jesus, and becomes at last an integrated personality, at peace with himself and with God. O'Neill, in 1934, appeared to have come to the end of his spiritual pilgrimage.

Actually, *Days without End* was a "mere interlude," as he admitted later, and did not reflect his personal religious convictions. For the moment he may have supposed that he could return to the Christian fold, but by 1939, when he wrote *The Iceman Cometh,* his mood had changed from tentative hope to unqualified despair. World War II was beginning, and the human race was obviously "too damned stupid" (this was O'Neill's phrase) to realize that its salvation depended on one "simple sentence": What shall it profit a man if he gain the whole world and lose his own soul? Perhaps, O'Neill told a reporter, mankind ought to be dumped down the nearest drain and the world given over to the ants.

These are hardly Christian sentiments, despite the quotation from the New Testament, and *The Iceman Cometh* cannot, therefore, have the same sort of religious significance as *Days without End*: it cannot be a Christian play. Can it be a recantation of the point of view of *Days without End?* Can it be, in any sense, a repudiation of Christianity?

Since O'Neill himself has given us the hint, let us begin our inquiry with the title. On the surface, the iceman is a reference to Hickey's ribald jest that he knows his wife is safe because he has left her with the iceman in the hay. On a "deeper" level, the iceman represents death, as O'Neill pointed out in 1946, and as Larry Slade points out in the play when he learns that Hickey's wife is dead. "It fits," Slade says, "for Death was the Iceman Hickey called to his home."

It is not enough, however, merely to identify the iceman with death. We must realize also that the iceman is the foil of the bridegroom of Scripture, and that he stands for the opposite of everything the bridegroom stands for. In the symbolism of theology, the bridegroom is always Christ, giver of life eternal. Waiting for the bridegroom symbolizes man's hope of redemption. Union with the bridegroom, conceived as a marriage, is the "final end and realized meaning" [1] of the life of every Christian, the "fulfillment of promise and [the] consummation of hope." Union with the bridegroom signifies victory over death and salvation in the world to come.

Union with the iceman, conceived as adultery, must, then, be a parody of union with the bridegroom, and signify surrender to death and acquiescence in personal annihilation. Evelyn Hickman, after her husband kills her, finds the peace of oblivion in the arms of the symbolical iceman. The other characters in the play will eventually find the same kind of peace when they abandon their illusory hope of happiness, whether here and now on earth, or in a hypothetical Christian hereafter.

Construed in this way, *The Iceman Cometh* (on one of its many levels of meaning) is seen to be a parable of the destiny of man. All men are waiting for the iceman, but only those who have shed their ultimate illusions are aware that the "final end and realized meaning" of their lives is death. "I'm the only real convert to death Hickey made here," says Slade, who speaks for O'Neill in the play. "From the bottom of my coward's heart I mean that now."

"I want to go to the chair," says Hickey, when he realizes that his love for his wife was an illusion, and that he killed her because he hated her. "Do you suppose I give a damn about life now?" he asks the detective who has arrested him. "Why, you bonehead, I haven't got a single damned lying hope or pipe dream left." The other derelicts in Hope's saloon (the world of illusions) lack Slade's philosophic detachment and Hickey's psychopathic insight, and are afraid to face

[1] See L. A. Zander's discussion of the problem of the bridegroom in his *Dostoevsky*, 1948, pp. 97-137.

the truth: that waiting for the iceman constitutes the chief employment of their futile lives.

The paradox of fulfillment through annihilation is a concept that O'Neill could have derived either from Schopenhauer or from Freud, who reached the conclusion previously reached by Schopenhauer, though by a different route, that the goal of life is death. The immediate stimulus to his imagination, however, may have been Waldo Frank's novel *The Bridegroom Cometh,* in which the heroine gives herself to a succession of bridegrooms, both spiritual (Christ, Freud, Marx) and material (a husband and several lovers). Only Marx satisfies her need for love, and in the end she finds fulfillment through identification with the masses. O'Neill, unlike Frank, never supposed that a political or sociological nostrum could cure the diseases of the soul.

A second key to O'Neill's attitude toward Christianity in *The Iceman Cometh* is the role of the hardware salesman Hickey. When the curtain rises on Act I, the derelicts in Hope's hotel, slumbering and sleeping in their chairs, are waiting for Hickey to visit them on one of his periodical benders. "Would that Hickey or Death would come," says Willie Oban. But Hickey has tarried: a prostitute has seen him standing at the next corner, and to her surprise he is sober.

"I kidded him," she says. " 'How's de iceman, Hickey? How's he doin' at your house?' He laughs and says, 'Fine.' And he says, 'Tell de gang I'll be along in a minute. I'm just finishin' figurin' out de best way to save dem and bring dem peace.' "

Hickey, when he arrives, is greeted by a very different cry from "Behold, the bridegroom cometh." "Here's the old son of a bitch," says Rocky; and "Bejees, Hickey, you old bastard, it's good to see you!" says Hope.

But Hickey is no longer the irresponsible drunkard the derelicts once knew and loved. He is on the wagon, and he proposes a stern remedy for what ails them. What he has to sell, in other words, is symbolical hardware, and he himself represents all self-appointed messiahs and saviors who meddle in other people's affairs and tell them how to live. Hence he can be fruitfully compared to Gregers Werle in Ibsen's *Wild Duck,* to Luka in Gorki's *Lower Depths,* and to the mysterious strangers in Jerome's *Passing of the Third Floor Back* and Kennedy's *Servant in the House.*

He also has something in common with Sigmund Freud, and his program of salvation is similar, in a general way, to psychoanalysis. He invites the derelicts to re-examine their pipe dreams (wish fulfillments) and to get rid of them by coming to terms with reality (the reality principle). This, he imagines, will make them happy. It doesn't, of course; and after their abortive attempts to resume their former occupations, they stagger back, demoralized and defeated, to the security of Hope's saloon. They cannot endure life unsupported by illusions, and instead of making them happy, Hickey deprives them of the will to live. Hickey has the last speech in each of the first three acts, and his last word in each is an ironical "happy." The notion that men can be happy in this worst of all possible worlds is an illusion.

Another illusion, or so Freud tells us, is religion. Man does not need its consolations, he says in *The Future of an Illusion,* nor can he remain a child forever. Rather he must venture out into the hostile world and be educated to reality. "Man can endure the cruelty of reality. What, you fear he will not stand the test? But it is at least something to know that one has been thrown on one's own resources."

This is very much like Hickey's program for the individual derelicts in *The Iceman Cometh.* Over and above their private illusions, however, stands Christianity, the collective illusion of what O'Neill thought of as our bankrupt Western civilization. Religion is an illusion, O'Neill evidently agreed; but unlike Freud, he did not think that the "swine called men" could live without it. Thus, by an extraordinary reconciliation of opposites, he equates the drunken Hickey with the secular savior Freud and the Christian Savior Christ, and at the same time rejects the gospels preached by both. Says Slade:

> Honor or dishonor, faith or treachery, are nothing but the opposites of the same stupidity which is ruler and king of life, and in the end they rot in the same grave. All things are the same meaningless joke to me, for they grin at me from the one skull of death.

That O'Neill had this anti-Christian undertone in mind when he compiled his medley of illusions in *The Iceman Cometh* is further substantiated by several tantalizing resemblances[2] between the play and the New Testament. Hickey as savior has twelve disciples. They drink wine at Hope's supper party, and their grouping on the stage, according to O'Neill's directions, is reminiscent of Leonardo da Vinci's painting of the Last Supper. Hickey leaves the party, as Christ does, aware that he is about to be executed. The three whores correspond in number to the three Marys, and sympathize with Hickey as the three Marys sympathize with Christ. (The implications of this resemblance are not without precedent: Christopher Marlowe, it will be recalled, was accused of saying that the women of Samaria were whores.)

One of the derelicts, Parritt, resembles Judas Iscariot in several ways. He is the twelfth in the list of *dramatis personae;* Judas is twelfth in the New Testament lists of the Disciples. He has betrayed his anarchist mother for a paltry $200; Judas betrayed Christ for

---

[2] First called to my attention by Mr. Philip Taylor.

thirty pieces of silver. He is from the far-away Pacific Coast; Judas was from far-away Judaea. Hickey reads his mind and motives; Christ read Judas's. Parritt compares himself to Iscariot when he says that his mother would regard anyone who quit the "Movement" as a Judas who ought to be boiled in oil. He commits suicide by jumping off a fire escape; Judas fell from a high place (Acts 1:18) or "hanged himself" (Matthew 27:5).

In the light of O'Neill's remarks concerning the Biblical and religious significance of his play, these resemblances can hardly be coincidental. They are no more than an undertone, to be sure—one of many undertones or subordinate layers of meaning—but they are consistent with the main theme of the play, and they account for some of its otherwise unaccountable features: for example, the emphasis on midnight (see Matthew 25:5-6) as the hour appointed for Hope's party, and the unnecessarily large number of derelicts in Hope's saloon. If O'Neill's only purpose had been to show that everyone, no matter how degraded, has one last pipe dream to sustain him, four or five derelicts, instead of twelve, would have sufficed, and the play would have been less redundant than, in fact, it is.

O'Neill was fond of hidden symbols and multiple layers of meaning. The nine acts of *Strange Interlude* and the name of the heroine, Nina, symbolize the nine months of a woman's pregnancy. Christine Mannon in *Mourning Becomes Electra* is called Christine (to correspond with Clytemnestra in Aeschylus's trilogy) instead of some other name beginning with "C" because O'Neill wanted to suggest that she is a sort of female anti-Christ or pagan martyr, crucified by a repressive Puritanism for her faith in sexuality. Lavinia Mannon is called Lavinia instead of a name beginning with "E" (to correspond with Electra) because "levin" means lightning or electricity. The name Mannon, from the last part of Agamemnon, suggests Mammon, the figurative divinity of all genuine Mannons. Examples of this sort of ingenuity, culled from other plays by O'Neill, could be multiplied indefinitely.

In addition to Hickey and Christine Mannon, O'Neill likens several other characters to Christ. In *The Fountain,* Bishop Menendez advises Juan to surrender the Indian Nano to the mob.

> Juan (*with wild scorn*). Ah, High Priest! Deliver him up, eh?
> Menendez. Juan! You are impious! (*Angrily*) It is sacrilege—to compare this Indian dog—you mock our Blessed Savior! You are cursed—I wash my hands—His will be done!

Nina, in *Strange Interlude,* cherishes the illusion that her dead lover Gordon Shaw is the real father of her son. "Immaculate conception,"

Marsden mutters in an unpublished manuscript version of the play.[3] "The Sons of the Father have all been failures!" Nina says, referring both to her son and to Christ. "Failing, they died for us . . . they could not stay with us, they could not give us happiness."

Allusions such as these abound in O'Neill's plays. *Where the Cross Is Made,* to cite a final example, contains what I surmise is a double reference to the sustaining power of illusions (the central theme, as we have seen, of *The Iceman Cometh*). As the curtain falls on the last scene, Nat Bartlett cries out with insane frenzy: "The treasure is buried where the cross is made." On the surface, this means that Nat, like his father, is obsessed by the belief that the trinkets on the island represent a fortune in gold. But the words also suggest that Christianity, symbolized by the Cross, is as much of an illusion as the gold. In view of the way he worked and thought, O'Neill cannot have been unaware of this implication of his title.

These considerations bring to mind an ironic scene in *The Great God Brown.* Dion Anthony, one of O'Neill's favorite characters and a recognizable self-portrait, designs a cathedral which, he boasts, is "one vivid blasphemy from the sidewalk to the tips of the spires!—but so concealed the fools will never know! They'll kneel and worship the ironic Silenus who tells them the best good is never to be born!"

When Brown inherits Dion's soul, he too introduces secret motifs into his work. Of a new state capitol that he designs, he says:

> Here's a wondrous fair Capitol! The design would do just as well for a Home for Criminal Imbeciles! Yet to them, such is my art, it will appear to possess a pure common sense, a fat-bellied finality, as dignified as the suspenders of an assemblyman. Only to me will that pompous façade reveal itself as the wearily ironic grin of Pan as he half listens to the laws passed by his fleas to enslave him.

Did O'Neill, in writing *The Iceman Cometh*—the question inevitably presents itself—did O'Neill do what Dion and Brown do in *The Great God Brown?* Did he, that is to say, introduce concealed blasphemies into his play, just as Dion and Brown introduce concealed blasphemies into their architectural designs? And did he laugh in secret at the critics who supposed that he had written a compassionate play in *The Iceman Cometh,* just as Dion and Brown laugh at the fools who do not see through their mockery?

André Malraux once asked if man in the twentieth century could survive after God had died in the nineteenth. O'Neill's answer in *The*

---

[3] Yale MS. 52, not at present available to scholars, but discussed by Miss Doris Alexander in her brilliant doctoral thesis entitled *Freud and O'Neill: An Analysis of Strange Interlude* (New York University, 1952).

Iceman Cometh is no. The derelicts in Hope's saloon, all of them childless, symbolize a humanity that is engaged in the laudable act of committing suicide. As the play ends, Larry Slade stares straight ahead (O'Neill's habitual way of depicting disillusionment) and waits for release from the intolerable burden of life. O'Neill's prolonged search for a faith had led him, not to faith, but to despair.

Could there have been in 1939, a more prophetic anticipation of the self-destructive compulsions of the Age of Nuclear Fission? Is there in dramatic literature a more nihilistic play than *The Iceman Cometh*?

The Iceman Cometh

by Doris Falk

In 1939, six years after *Days Without End*, O'Neill completed *The Iceman Cometh*, in 1940-41, *Long Day's Journey Into Night*, and in 1943, *A Moon for the Misbegotten* and *A Touch of the Poet*. During the same general period—from about 1934 to 1943—O'Neill had been hard at work on two long cycles of plays to be called *A Tale of Possessors Self-Dispossessed* and *By Way of Obit*. Of the first cycle he completed first drafts of three double-length plays, *The Greed of the Meek, And Give Me Death,* and *More Stately Mansions*. Dissatisfied with the early drafts of these plays and too ill to undertake drastic revision, O'Neill destroyed the first two. Although he had intended the destruction also of *More Stately Mansions*, a typescript of that play survives (the manuscript version was destroyed with the other two plays). Of the second cycle, *By Way of Obit*, O'Neill completed only one one-act play, entitled *Hughie*, still extant but unpublished.

At one time O'Neill had placed *A Touch of the Poet* fifth in the *Possessors* cycle, but when he abandoned the latter he considered his last four plays to be a related series, arranged in the following order: *The Iceman Cometh, A Moon for the Misbegotten, A Touch of the Poet,* and *Long Day's Journey Into Night*. The exact composition dates of these and the cycle plays are far from clear; some had begun years before—*A Touch of the Poet* in 1928. We do know, however, that between completion of *Days Without End* and this final group of plays about ten years had elapsed in which O'Neill's thinking underwent a change that reflected the frustrations of the intervening years.

O'Neill returned in these last plays to acceptance of struggle and flight as inseparable from and intrinsic to the life process. Now there is no way out but death. The struggle in these plays is essentially the same as it had always been in his work: the conscious intellect at war with the unconscious drives, the laceration of love and hate in every

"The Iceman Cometh" (*Original title: "Fatal Balance"*). From Eugene O'Neill and the Tragic Tension, *by Doris Falk (New Brunswick, N.J.: Rutgers University Press, 1958), pp. 156-64. Copyright © 1958 by Rutgers, the State University. Reprinted by permission of the publisher.*

close human relationship, and the desperate search for self among the masks. Flight from the struggle is still in the pursuit of one of these illusory masks—but here we see a difference.

At last O'Neill had come face to face with the inevitable question: What happens when, long before the end of the play, the fugitive becomes clearly conscious that flight is futile and the self-image false? When he learns that *all* self-images are illusions, and that furthermore they are projected by a self which is worthless, if it exists at all? Then the self and its ideal are equal—and both equal to zero. Instead of a pull from the self to the self-conception, resulting in action (wasteful though that action may be), we have a perfect equilibrium, resulting in paralysis. Then, indeed,

> . . . the odds is gone,
> And there is nothing left remarkable
> Beneath the visiting moon.

The theme of *The Iceman Cometh* is the death that results—the "iceman" who comes—when the self-images which keep the characters alive become known to them as mirage. The action takes place in "Hope's back room," the back room and a section of the bar of Harry Hope's saloon. Here fifteen derelicts keep themselves alive on alcohol and the "pipe dream" that they have been or some day will be respectable. They all know, at least unconsciously, the truth about themselves and each other, but they know, too, the vital necessity of illusion. So each accepts the other at his own evaluation and demands the same acceptance. As long as this state of things persists, as it does throughout the first act (nearly half the play), the characters are treated as comic. Their self-deceptions are ridiculous but not unlovable affectations. It is in the second act that, as O'Neill said, "the comedy breaks up and the tragedy comes on."

The commentator on the action and the actual protagonist of the play is Larry Slade, an aging ex-Anarchist who has long since withdrawn from the Movement and from life. In Act I Larry is comparatively happy. He has an image of himself as the philosopher-bum who observes life from the grandstand and waits only for death. He is proud that he can see what the others cannot: that "the lie of a pipe-dream is what gives life to the whole misbegotten mad lot of us, drunk or sober. . . . Mine are all dead and buried behind me. What's before me is the comforting fact that death is a fine long sleep and I'm damned tired, and it can't come too soon for me." (Act I, *Plays*, III, p. 578.)

Yet, Larry's final disillusionment is still to come, in the person of young Parritt, the eighteen-year-old ex-Anarchist who has betrayed the Movement and his own mother, whom Larry once loved. (In fact, the context hints that Parritt is Larry's son.) Disillusion comes for the others in the person of Hickey (Theodore Hickman), the traveling salesman whose success they all envy.

Hickey arrives at the bar on Harry Hope's birthday, an occasion for one of his periodical binges, but instead of the gay and dissolute Hickey they all expect, he is serious and sober. He announces the reason for the change: He has at last found peace by facing the truth about himself. Gradually he shames his listeners into believing that they, too, will find peace if they destroy their illusions and see themselves as they really are. He persuades all except Larry to go forth into the daylight and attempt the social rehabilitation they have always promised themselves. One by one, however, they crawl back to the bar the next day, broken and defeated by inevitable failure. They have faced the truth, but it has robbed them of the last, pitiful trace of hope.

Now not even liquor can make them happy; their old friendships turn to antagonisms. Hickey realizes that his plan has failed, and in trying to explain the failure to himself and to them he reveals that he attained his state of "peace" by killing his wife, Evelyn.

Hickey has convinced himself that he killed his wife because he loved her and wanted to spare her unhappiness over his uncontrollable drunkenness and dissipation—but as he speaks, his real motive comes through. He hated Evelyn because no matter what he did she always forgave him, never punished him, was always faithful. His running gag with the boys at Hope's had been that Evelyn was betraying him "in the hay with the iceman," but this was only his own wishful thinking. She never gave him even this relief from his own guilt. Hickey killed Evelyn because that was the only way he could free himself from her eternal forgiveness and achieve the ultimate in self-punishment. For him, to commit murder was to commit suicide. He has already called the police at the time of his confession.

When the police have arrived, however, and Hickey is concluding his story, his guilt becomes too much for him to face. Ironically, he creates his own pipe dream by persuading himself that he was insane at the moment of the murder. Hickey's illusion is a blessing to his friends, for it restores their own. Now they can go back to their bottles, convinced that they knew Hickey was insane all the time and faced reality only to humor him.

But Larry cannot go back. He must listen to Parritt's confessions— in dramatic antiphony to Hickey's—of his hatred of his mother (caused chiefly by jealousy of her many lovers) which led him to betray her to life imprisonment. Parritt has already resolved upon suicide, but he forces Larry to support his resolution. After listening to Parritt's outpourings, Larry finally cries, "Go, get the hell out of life,

God damn you, before I choke it out of you! . . ." Parritt is relieved
and grateful: "Thanks, Larry. I just wanted to be sure. I can see now
it's the only possible way I can ever get free from her. . . . It ought
to comfort Mother a little, too. . . . She'll be able to say, 'Justice is
done! So may all traitors die!' . . ."

The mother-spirit has destroyed another of her sons.

When Larry hears Parritt fall from the fire escape, "A long forgotten
faith returns to him for a moment. . . ." At least Parritt had the
courage of his conviction. But the death of Parritt is the death of
Larry's last illusion about himself. "He opens his eyes—with a bitter
self-derision." He is no longer the philosopher, but only another
down-and-out bum.

> Be God, there's no hope! I'll never be a success in the grandstand—or
> anywhere else! Life is too much for me! I'll be a weak fool looking
> with pity at the two sides of everything till the day I die! . . . Be God,
> I'm the only real convert to death Hickey made here. From the bottom
> of my coward's heart I mean that now! (Act IV, *Plays*, III, pp. 726-727.)

The objectivist (as Larry thought he was at first), who looks at
both sides of everything until they have equal value, must be a
paralyzed spectator, unable to take action in any direction; but when
the "two sides" are the masks of himself and both are worthless illusions, perfectly balanced against each other, he is not even a paralyzed
spectator; he is dead. In *The Iceman Cometh*, as in the earlier plays,
life and the self are lost together, when the tragic tension between the
selves is lost.

The two sides of himself that Larry has seen are his expansive and
submissive self-images. The expansive is that of the Anarchist, the
active participator in "the Movement." The submissive is seen in his
drive toward self-destruction. If Larry had been able to give either
of these selves the value of a reality, he would have been drawn toward one or toward the other, would have been able to act either in
the direction of his political obligations or in the direction of death
by suicide, as Parritt did. Since he is pulled in both directions at once,
he can only withdraw from the struggle altogether and become a non-
participating observer of himself as well as of life. In Jung's terms,
Larry exemplifies the "equal distribution of psychic energy." In
Horney's, he is the neurotic who finds a pseudosolution to conflict in
"resignation: the appeal of freedom." When Larry himself discovers
the unreality of his solution, there is nothing left for him but the living death which Kierkegaard called "the disconsolateness of not being
able to die." Even his conception of physical death as a warm and
comforting womb (the return to the Earth Mother) or as a Babylon
where " 'tis cool beneath thy willow tree" is to him only another illu-

sion. Nevertheless, death is the single solution to his dilemma, since only annihilation of the self can annihilate the dilemma. His very inability to propel himself actively toward this annihilation—to accomplish it through suicide—is also death.

The philosophical implications of Larry's position are just as interesting as the psychological. Behind Aristotle's ethical definition of character as "that which reveals moral purpose, showing what kind of things a man chooses or avoids," is the problem which exists in some degree for every self-aware person, as it does in the extreme for the neurotic: the problem of creating oneself, of forming one's own character. The preliminaries and the process of choosing, even though they may be unconscious, are as important as the choice itself and the responsibility which is its result. Larry's power of choice is brought to a standstill because he cannot accomplish the preparation for it. His is the problem of projecting value in a world devoid of absolutes —the "existential" dilemma: man's chief struggle is not with Something but with Nothing, not with Evil but with the valuelessness that is neither good nor evil. Once he has overcome this Nothing, has created his values, man is then free to act according to them (or even, knowingly, contrary to them), but he is completely responsible both for the values and the actions predicated upon them. Such utter self-contingency can be paralyzing; it provides freedom, but it is that terrifying freedom from which, as Erich Fromm points out, most of us feel compelled to escape.

In defense of this philosophy as a "humanism" Sartre has pointed out that it is as positive as it is negative—as hopeful as it is despairing —in that each man has not only the responsibility, but the opportunity, to create his own destiny, and that each individual is ultimately responsible for the destiny of mankind as a whole. O'Neill has not only placed Larry in the existential dilemma, but has made him see and live both sides of the dilemma itself. In his youth Larry dedicated himself to Anarchism, an affirmation of nothingness and chaos and of man's freedom to create his destiny; but in his old age he sees anarchy's opposite face, that negation which we call despair.

The Iceman Cometh

by Robert Brustein

In *Ah Wilderness!*, romanticized sex and half-baked philosophy, finally, are the enthusiasms of a character who is an adolescent himself; and, as a result, the play marks a turning point in O'Neill's relation to his material. If *Days Without End* suggests a new detachment towards his religious questing, *Ah Wilderness!* prefigures his transformation into an objective dramatic artist. As his self-awareness grows, O'Neill is beginning to distance himself from dogma and opinions. In the mouth of the seventeen-year-old Romantic Richard Miller, the author's familiar paeans to Beauty, Love, and Life seem perfectly acceptable, since O'Neill is treating these affirmations with gentle satire and indulgent whimsy. It is the character, not the author, who is now identified with *fin de siècle* pessimism, culled from Swinburne, Nietzsche, and Omar Khayyam, just as it is the character, not the author, who is inclined to sentimentalize prostitutes. The play, in short, has finally become more important than the theme—ideas are effectively subordinated to "the experience in which they are implied." By projecting his literary self-consciousness onto an earlier Self, O'Neill is beginning to free himself from it. And in *Ah Wilderness!*, he exposes previously suppressed talents for depicting the habitual and commonplace side of existence, along with unsuspected gifts for portraying the humorous side of Irish family life.

Ah Wilderness!, to be sure, is an exercise for the left hand—a sentimental piece of Americana written in a holiday mood—but it is less important in itself than for what it portends: O'Neill is preparing to strike out along new paths. The author himself seems perfectly conscious of a new departure in this play, because, in a letter to Lawrence Langner, he couples it with *Days Without End* as evidence of his growing self-understanding: "For, after all, this play [*Days Without End*], like *Ah Wilderness!* but in a much deeper sense, is the paying of an old debt on my part—a gesture toward more compre-

"The Iceman Cometh" [*editor's title*] by Robert Brustein. From The Theatre of Revolt *(Boston and Toronto: Atlantic-Little, Brown and Company, 1965), pp. 336-48. Copyright © 1962, 1963, 1964 by Robert Brustein. Reprinted by permission of the publisher.*

hensive, unembittered understanding and inner freedom—the breaking away from an old formula that I had enslaved myself with. . . ."
What the "old formula" is we have already seen; O'Neill's new approach is to leave all formulae behind, and relax into the role of the
artist. Psychologically, O'Neill's bitterness towards authority seems
to have left him, along with his restless quest for absolutes; philosophically, he has begun to perceive the hollowness of his messianic
pretensions, and to turn towards material which he has pulled out of
his being rather than self-consciously adopted; thematically, he has
abandoned myths of incest and romantic love for deeper probes of
character; formally, he is learning to combine the solipsistic subjec-
tivity of Strindberg with the more detached, ordered, and indirectly
biographical approach of Ibsen. Instead of writing about his unas-
similated present, O'Neill is beginning to root about in the experiences of his past, and to do so with patience and care. After producing at least one play a year from 1913 to 1933 (in 1920, he wrote
four), O'Neill considerably slows his output, completing only four
full-length works and one short play in the next twenty years.

Ah Wilderness! is like all the plays which are to follow in being a
work of recollection—nostalgic and retrospective. And significantly,
it does not contain a trace of Expressionism, being surprisingly conventional in technique and structure. Later, O'Neill is to develop a
different kind of realism all his own, built on a centripetal pattern in
which a series of repetitions bring us closer and closer to the explosion
at the center; but *Ah Wilderness!* is typical of O'Neill's late plays in
its avoidance of conspicuous formal experimentation. Masks, split
characters, and choruses are gone forever. As a result, O'Neill aban-
dons those ponderous abstractions and inflated generalizations which
Expressionism invariably dragged into his plays. If the author once
complained, about *The Hairy Ape,* that "the public saw just the
stoker, not the symbol, and the symbol makes the play either important or just another play," then he is now able to subordinate symbolism, and sometimes suppress it entirely for the sake of penetrating
studies of character.

O'Neill, in short, has finally discovered where his true talents lie.
In 1924, in the act of eulogizing Strindberg, he had called Ibsen a
"lesser man," attacking Ibsenite realism in these terms: "It represents
our Fathers' daring aspirations towards self-recognition by holding the
family kodak up to ill-nature . . . we have endured too much from
the banality of surfaces." Less embittered towards "our Fathers"
nine years later, O'Neill is beginning to create a drama of surface
banality himself—beneath which the forces of destruction will proceed with Ibsenite inevitability—and it is precisely the "family
kodak" which will be O'Neill's artistic instrument. As John Henry

Raleigh has observed about one of these late plays, "Everything pales beside the fact of the *family*, which is the macro-microcosm that blots out the universe. . . ." The family becomes the nucleus of every major work that follows, except *The Iceman Cometh*, and even there, the characters are thrown together into a kind of accidental family group. As for the unfinished cycle, this was inspired by O'Neill's desire to follow his family further and further into the past: "The Cycle is primarily that," he writes to Langner, "the history of a family. What larger significance I can give my people as extraordinary examples and symbols in the drama of American possessiveness and materialism is something else again." In *Ah Wilderness!*, O'Neill develops a hazy daguerreotype of Irish family life at the turn of the century; but before long, the family kodak will focus on the author's most painful early memories, seen with consuming power and ruthless honesty, yet with compassion, understanding, and love.

O'Neill's retrospective technique is admirably illustrated in *The Iceman Cometh* (1939), where O'Neill closes the door forever on his messianic ambitions, and the suffering artist becomes completely identified with the structured art. "*The Iceman* is a denial of any other experience of faith in my plays," he remarks, soon after completing the play. "In writing it, I felt I had locked myself in with my memories." At first glance, the author's place in these memories is obscure, for the play does not look very autobiographical. Harry Hope's saloon is based on Jimmy-the-Priest's, a West-Side rooming bar that O'Neill used to frequent in his youth—("Gorky's Night Lodgings," he was later to remark, "was an ice cream parlor in comparison," and the influence of Gorky is certainly evident in the seedy, peeled, splotched setting, and the dissipated characters)[1] and the play contains thinly veiled portraits of some of the derelicts the author used to know there and at another saloon called the Hell Hole. But although the work is set in 1912, the same climacteric year as *A Long Day's Journey*, the author himself is simply a lens through which the characters are seen. Still, if O'Neill is not the central character of the play, romanticized as a mocking, sardonic rebel, he is still present in disguise—partly in two characters, as we shall see, but mostly as a guide through the caverns of his deepest perceptions. O'Neill here is using his "memories" not for personal autobiography in the manner of Strindberg, but in the manner of Ibsen, for spiritual and psychological autobiography. As the author himself says, *The Iceman Cometh* is a repudiation of "any other experience of faith in

[1] For an analysis of Gorky's influence on the play, see Helen Muchnic's article, "The Irrelevancy of Belief: The Iceman and the Lower Depths," in *O'Neill and His Plays*, edited by Oscar Cargill, N. Bryllion Fagin, and William J. Fisher.

my plays." In denying his previous philosophical affirmations, he permits a terrible sense of reality to rise to consciousness.

In its repudiation of past faith, *The Iceman Cometh* occupies much the same place in O'Neill's work as *The Wild Duck* does in Ibsen's; and, indeed, the two plays have more in common even than this positioning. The theme of *The Iceman*—that men cannot live without illusions—is so close to the theme of *The Wild Duck*[2] that some critics have been inclined to dismiss the later play as a mere recapitulation of the earlier one. This is a mistake. O'Neill's play, to my mind, is a greater achievement than Ibsen's, and it certainly has a different emphasis. In *The Wild Duck,* it is morally wrong to rob people of their life-lies; in *The Iceman Cometh,* it is *tragic.* Gregers Werle is a satire on pseudo-Ibsenites who meddle in the lives of others, urging the claim of some impossible ideal, but Theodore Hickman is not a vicarious idealist but a realist, and one who believes he has pragmatically tested the kind of salvation he is pressing on his friends. Although Gregers is misguided, and Hjalmar Ekdal is inadequate to his demands, Ibsen still believes there are heroic individuals (Brand and Stockman, for example) with the courage to face the unclothed truth. But the whole world is inadequate to Hickey's demands, for the truth he offers is a naked, blinding light which kills. Thus, *The Wild Duck* is a savage indictment of some men; *The Iceman Cometh* is a compassionate insight into all. O'Neill is reflecting not ethically, on Right Action or Right Thought, but metaphysically, on the very quality of existence. And, as a result, he is finally working through experientially to that tragic mood so self-consciously imposed on his earlier work.

Because he is universalizing Ibsen's theme, O'Neill has created instead of one antagonist a whole catalogue of them—the deadbeats, alcoholics, pimps, whores, bartenders, and illusionists who inhabit Harry Hope's premises. The proliferation of characters adds greatly to the length of the play, which is bulky and unwieldy in the extreme; and since each character is identified by a single obsession which he continually restates, the play is extremely repetitious as well. Thus, despite the naturalistic setting, the play is much too schematic to qualify as a convincing evocation of reality. Each act offers a single variation on the theme of illusion; the action never bursts into spontaneous life; and the characters rarely transcend their particular functions. A thematic realism rather than an atmospheric realism prevails; O'Neill seems reluctant to let the play escape his rigid control. One

---

[2] It is also very close to the theme of Pirandello's plays, though O'Neill differs from the Italian dramatist in believing that objective reality can still be reached through the human mind.

must concede that there is some justice in Eric Bentley's objection: "There are ideas in the play, and we have the impression that what should be the real substance of it is mere (not always deft) contrivance to illustrate the ideas." Still, O'Neill's ideas, for once, proceed logically from the action, and, for once, they are totally convincing. I do not think Professor Bentley properly appreciates the depth, sincerity, and relevance of O'Neill's dramatic insights in this play.

Professor Bentley detects padding and recommends cuts; O'Neill's Broadway director, Paul Crabtree, also suggested cuts on the basis that O'Neill has made the same point eighteen times—"I intended to be repeated eighteen times," the playwright said, and refused to tamper with the play. O'Neill was right; cutting would undoubtedly diminish the impact of the work. For once, an O'Neill play is long not because the author knows too little but rather because he knows too much; even the repetitions are an intricate aspect of the total design. O'Neill has multiplied his antagonists in order to illuminate every aspect of his theme, just as he has drawn them from the humblest condition of life in order to show mankind at the extremity of its fate. Dazed by alcohol, isolated from human society, O'Neill's derelicts are stripped of every pretension except the single "pipe dream" that keeps them going, and the sum of these pipe dreams is meant to represent the total content of human illusion.

Thus, Hugo's aristocratic will to power through pretended love of the proletariat reflects on political illusions; Joe's pugnacious demand for equality with the whites, on racial illusions; Chuck and Cora's fantasy of marriage and a farm, on domestic illusions; the prostitutes' mysterious distinction between "tarts" and "whores," on status illusions; Parritt's false motives for having betrayed his mother, on psychological illusions; Willie Oban's excuse for having discontinued law school, on intellectual illusions; Larry Slade's pretense at disillusionment and detachment, on philosophical illusions—and Hickey's belief that he has found salvation, on religious illusions. All of these dreamers represent a family of men, inextricably bound up with each other. Each is able to see the lie of the other without being able to admit his own, but in this community, the price of mutual toleration is mutual silence. Actually, the community is almost Utopian. Before Hickey comes, the men live in relative harmony together by adhering to a single doctrine—the doctrine of Tomorrow—keeping hope alive through the anticipation of significant action on a day which never comes.

Against the Tomorrow doctrine, Hickey counterposes his doctrine of Today, forcing the derelicts to execute their dreams—and fail them—on the assumption that a life without illusions is a life without guilt. In this conflict of ideologies, Hickey's main antagonist is Larry

Slade, the intellectual champion of the Tomorrowmen, who is brought into the lists against his conscious will. Playing the part of the "Old Grandstand Foolosopher," pretending indifference to the fate of his companions, Larry has adopted a mask of total alienation. For him, the essence of mankind is excrement, and life on earth is doomed: "The material the ideal society must be constructed from is men themselves," he observes, explaining his apostasy from Anarchism, "and you can't build a marble temple out of mud and manure." "Old Cemetery," as he is called, is aroused only by the thought of death, and affects to contemplate his own with pleasurable anticipation. But although he pretends "a bitter, cynic philosophy," as Jimmy Tomorrow observes, "in your heart, you are the kindest man among us." Actually, Larry is doomed to inaction by a reflective intelligence which always sees both sides of a question, and he is forever trying to suppress his instinctive compassion. O'Neill describes him as "a pitying but weary old priest." He has heard all the secrets of the confessional, and out of his secret kindness is desperately trying to protect these secrets, including his own, from Hickey's remorseless efforts to bring them into light. Harry Hope's may be "Bedrock Bar, The End of the Line Cafe, The Bottom of the Sea Rathskeller," but it has "a beautiful calm in the atmosphere" which can only be preserved if it is not touched by truth.

Hickey, however, finds this a false calm, and desires to introduce a genuine spiritual peace: "All I want," he says, using a word which ironically concludes every act but the last, "is to see you *happy*." But while Hickey is convinced that only truth brings peace, Larry knows that happiness is based exclusively on mutual deception: "To hell with the truth! As the history of the world proves, the truth has no bearing on anything. . . . The lie of a pipe dream is what gives life to the whole misbegotten mad lot of us, drunk or sober." This tension between truth and illusion reflects, in much stronger dramatic terms, O'Neill's former antithesis of Nietzschean heroism and Christian compassion. But instead of forcing a synthesis, as he does in his messianic plays, O'Neill rejects the heroic teachings of Nietzsche, repudiating superhuman salvation while affirming humanity, pity, and love. Together, Hickey and Larry function in somewhat the same way as the split characters of O'Neill's earlier work; but having relinquished his messianic claims, O'Neill is able to treat both aspects of his personality with a good deal more balance and equanimity. Thus, Larry's facile pessimism, his cynicism, and his fascination with death are all qualities found in O'Neill's earlier "sardonic" heroes, but these are now exposed as mere attitudinizing. And Hickey's evangelism represents the messianic impulse in O'Neill turned back on itself, for his gospel of truth is revealed as the greatest illusion of all.

The Iceman Cometh, then, is about the impossibility of salvation in a world without God, an expression of existential revolt structured in quasi-religious terms. And beneath the realistic surface, O'Neill is developing an ironic Christian parable, in a surprisingly subtle manner. For one thing, Hickey's entrance is delayed so long that—like another long-awaited figure, Beckett's Godot—he begins to accumulate supernatural qualities. "Would that Hickey or Death would come," moans one impatient character—an anticipatory irony, since Hickey will soon be identified with Death. Hickey finally does arrive, but the amiable jester has undergone a startling transformation. "I'm damned sure he's brought death with him," remarks Larry. "I feel the cold touch of it on him." The recurrent iceman motif intensifies these associations. On each of his annual visits, Hickey has joked that his chaste wife, Evelyn, was in the hay with the iceman; and as the derelicts grow more and more tormented by Hickey's penetrating thrusts, their one hope is that the joke has come to roost. And indeed it has, though not in the manner they think. Evelyn is now being held in a frigid embrace; Hickey, we finally learn, has murdered her; "Death was the Iceman Hickey called to his home." Thus, Hickey, Death, and the Iceman are one. The truth doesn't set you free, it kills you dead; the peace which Hickey brings to Harry Hope's saloon is the peace of the grave. Hickey, therefore, is the false Messiah—not the Resurrection and the Life, but the "great Nihilist," starting "a movement which will blow up the world."

To emphasize his anti-messianic point, O'Neill has hidden parallels with another great world movement, Christianity, throughout the play. And Cyrus Day has done us the service of uncovering most of them in his article, "The Iceman and the Bridegroom":

> Hickey as savior has twelve disciples. They drink wine at Hope's supper party, and their grouping on the stage, according to O'Neill's directions, is reminiscent of Leonardo da Vinci's painting of the Last Supper. Hickey leaves the party, as Christ does, aware that he is about to be executed. The three whores correspond in number to the three Marys, and sympathize with Hickey as the three Marys sympathize with Christ. . . . One of the derelicts, Parritt, resembles Judas Iscariot in several ways. He is twelfth in the list of dramatis personae; Judas is twelfth in the New Testament of the Disciples. He has betrayed his anarchist mother for a paltry $200; Judas betrayed Christ for thirty pieces of silver. . . .

To this list of striking resemblances, we might add another interesting one. Larry Slade becomes the only real convert to Hickey's religion of Death—he is, like Saint Peter, the rock on which Hickey builds his Church.

The symbolic aspect of the play, however, is not very obtrusive, if indeed it is noticeable at all without the aid of a commentator. On a purely denotative level, the work is still very rich. O'Neill has carefully combined Hickey's symbolic role as a false Messiah with his family background and psychological history, so that Hickey stands as a full-bodied character on his own, and a much more convincing salesman figure than Miller's Willy Loman (at least we know what Hickey sells—hardware). The son of a minister, Hickey has brought an evangelical fervor to the drummer's trade, and the techniques of salesmanship to his evangelism. In a country where everything is bought and sold, O'Neill is suggesting, even a religious vision must be peddled. Bruce Barton's observation that Jesus was a super-salesman may be in the back of O'Neill's mind; Billy Graham's religious "crusades" come immediately to ours. Hickey certainly employs the "hard sell"—cheery, good-humored, loud, brash, and pitiless—bearing down on his victim like Major Barbara bringing God to Bill Walker, or a psychoanalyst unearthing the source of a patient's neurosis. He has an instinctual eye for human weakness, partly because of his own experience ("I've had hell inside me. I can spot it in others"), but partly because he is "The Great Salesman" and can detect the vulnerability of a client in an instant.

As a result of this native shrewdness, Hickey has, by the end of the second act, transformed all the derelicts into caged animals, snarling at each other in their agony: each is beginning to open the other's wounds in order to protect his own, and even the goodnatured Harry Hope has developed an uncharacteristic pugnacity. Torn from the security of their dreams, the derelicts must now confront their To-morrow, each performing the deed which terrifies him most. The third act takes place in cold, daylight horror. The derelicts are afflicted with the "katzenjammers," their withdrawal symptoms aggravated by a growing apprehensiveness. Harry Hope, symbolizing the communal predicament, prepares at last to walk around the ward—but is unable even to cross the street. His illusion exposed, Harry's hope vanishes, and with it the hope of all his companions: only blank, unstructured reality remains. Having abandoned hope, the men are dwelling in hell; even the alcohol has lost its punch; all escape routes are closed. What results is death-in-life: "Vhat's matter, Harry?" asks Hugo. "You look funny. You look dead." Hugo's babbling, and the growling of the derelicts, turns the atmosphere funereal. Hickey's salvation is failing, and so is Hickey's confidence: "That's what worries me about you, Governor," he says to Harry, as the expected peace fails to come. "It's time you began to feel happy—"

In the last act, the derelicts have turned to stone, their spirits calcified by the death ray of truth. Motivated by growing nervousness over their behavior, Hickey begins his long speech of confession—

a confession which is also a discovery—paralleled by an antiphonal speech from Parritt. Both have destroyed a woman; both for reasons that they cannot face. Parritt has informed on his mother not out of patriotism or penury but rather out of hatred; and Hickey has killed Evelyn because she killed his joy of life, filling him with guilt through constant forgiveness of his sins. Thus, Hickey's act was an act of revenge and not of love; he not only hated her illusion, he detested her. As he blurts out, in the unconsidered slip which gives him away, "You know what you can do with your pipe dream now, you damned bitch."

Hickey can admit this feeling to his consciousness only for a moment; then, he immediately pleads insanity. "Good God, I couldn't have said that! If I did, I'd gone insane! Why, I loved Evelyn better than anything in life." It is this plea which leads Eric Bentley to say that "O'Neill's eye was off the subject":

> Not being clearly seen, the man is unclearly presented to the audience; O'Neill misleads them for several hours, then asks them to reach back into their memory and re-interpret all Hickey's actions and attitudes from the beginning. Is Hickey the character O'Neill needed as the man who tries to deprive the gang of their illusions? He (as it turns out) is a maniac. But if the attempt to disillude the gang is itself mad, it would have more dramatic point made by a sane idealist (as in *The Wild Duck*).

I cite this passage because it contains a widely shared misunderstanding of the play which has obscured its real profundity. For the fact is, of course, that O'Neill's eye remained steadfastly on the subject: Hickey, consistent in conception from first to last, is not a maniac at all. Actually, he only claims to have been insane at the time of the murder, but even this is a self-deception which he adopts so as not to face his real feelings towards his wife. Such a conclusion is clear enough from the context, and Parritt suggests it even more bluntly in the course of his own confession: "*And I'm not putting up any bluff either, that I was crazy afterwards* when I laughed to myself and thought, 'You know what you can do with your freedom pipe dream now, don't you, you damned old bitch!'" [My emphasis]. Hickey's plea of insanity, in short, is a bluff—not to escape the chair (he wants to die now) but to escape the truth: he cannot admit that he hated his wife. In a context like this, as a matter of fact, Hickey's mental state is totally irrelevant, since even madness is an escape from an unpleasant reality; the point is that Hickey, who thought he was living the truth, was living another pipe dream. As for the derelicts, they are willing to believe that Hickey was mad, because this means he told them lies; if he will agree to let them have their illusions, they will agree to let him have his. Hickey hesitates because he knows he told them the truth, but for the sake of his own peace, he must agree to the trade. Thus, he enters their community at last: mutual toleration through mutual silence.

Hickey's brand of salvation, in short, has proved of false manufacture: the happiness he discovered after Evelyn's death was merely the happiness of another illusion. Thus, his attempt to "disillude the gang" is not "itself mad," it is simply based on a terrible error; and since his own illusions are directly implicated in the action, Hickey has a good deal *more* dramatic point than Gregers Werle. Hickey, in fact, has some of the dimension of a tragic protagonist, and is brought right up to the brink of a tragic perception; if he does not look over, then Larry Slade does, and what he sees is the bottomless abyss of a totally divested reality:

> Be God, there's no hope. I'll never be a success in the grandstand—or anywhere else! Life is too much for me! I'll be a weak fool looking with pity at the two sides of everything till the day I die! (*With an intense bitter sincerity*) May that day come soon! (*He pauses startledly, surprised himself—then with a sardonic grin*) Be God, I'm the only real convert to death Hickey made here. From the bottom of my coward's heart I mean that now!

Hickey has escaped reality by pleading insanity; Parritt by committing suicide; the derelicts by returning to their illusions. But for Larry, too truthful to lie and too cowardly to die, the abyss is constantly before his eyes. Out of compassion for the Judas, Parritt, he has told him to put an end to his miserable existence; and now he must bear responsibility for this and every act until his own life ends: "May that day come soon!" His desire for death is like that of Othello: "For, in my sense, 'tis happiness to die." The play ends in laughter, song, and the drunken babble of Hugo, as Larry stares straight ahead of him, a living corpse, swathed in the winding sheet of truth. Like O'Neill's, his tragic posturing has developed finally into a deeply experienced tragic sense of life.

This extraordinary play, then, is a chronicle of O'Neill's own spiritual metamorphosis from a messianic into an existential rebel, the shallow yea-saying salvationist of the earlier plays having been transformed into a penetrating analyst of human motive rejecting even the pose of disillusionment. O'Neill's "denial of any other experience of faith in my plays" has left him alone, at last, with existence itself; and he has looked at it with a courage which only the greatest tragic dramatists have been able to muster. *The Iceman Cometh*, despite its prosaic language, recreates that existential groan which is heard in Shakespeare's tragedies and in the third choral poem of Sophocles's *Oedipus at Colonus*, as O'Neill makes reality bearable through the metaphysical consolations of art. O'Neill has rejected Hickey's brand of salvation as a way to human happiness, but truth has, nevertheless, become the cornerstone of his drama, truth combined with the compassionate understanding of Larry Slade. Expunging everything false and literary from his work, O'Neill has finally reconciled himself to being the man he really is.

The Irrelevancy of Belief:
The Iceman and *The Lower Depths*

by *Helen Muchnic*

When in *The Odyssey* the companions of Odysseus are changed
by Circe into swine, they are not deprived of human consciousness;
but in Milton's reworking of the episode in *Comus* the men are transformed so thoroughly that they have lost all notion of what has happened to them, and are completely brutish and contented in their
pleasures. Milton, that is, in a way consistent with the severity of
Puritanism, changed the pathos of a state in which human beings
suffer from a sense of their depravity into the greater moral tragedy
of a condition so depraved as to make such suffering impossible.[1]
Eugene O'Neill's *The Iceman Cometh* and Maxim Gorky's *The
Lower Depths* are, it seems to me, a modern instance of much the same
contrast. But, although a comparison of these two plays seems clearly
indicated, the fullest one that I have seen so far is but a brief discussion
in the Russian journal *Zvezda*[2]; there, in the course of a long, and
generally scornful, article on current American literature, Vladimir
Rubin concludes that, "If Gorky's play asserts: 'Man—that has a proud
sound,' then O'Neill's *The Iceman Cometh* seems to be saying: 'Man
—that has a low and infamous sound,' for "the gloomy moral" of his
play "debases man infinitely . . . as a pitiful, will-less toy of fate."
It marks, he says, "the final 'spiritual capitulation' of this veteran of
American drama." This, of course, is the opinion one would expect
from Soviet criticism today; and there is, to be sure, a shade of truth
in it. By comparison with Gorky's view of man, O'Neill's is indeed a
pessimistic one. But this shadowy truth dismisses with too casual a
brutality the realms of concepts here involved. The whole matter is

---

"*The Irrelevancy of Belief:* The Iceman *and* The Lower Depths" [*Original title:*
"*Circe's Swine: Plays by Gorky and O'Neill*"], *by Helen Muchnic. From* Comparative
Literature, *III* (*Spring, 1951*), *119-28. Copyright* © *by* Comparative Literature.
Reprinted by permission of the editor.

[1] This comparison was made some years ago by Marjorie Nicolson in one of her
lectures at Smith College.

[2] Aug. 1948, p. 200.

deeper and of a different order than that indicated by Mr. Rubin's remarks.

On the face of it, the plays are very much alike, not only in setting, plot, and structure, but in aesthetic conception; for they seem to be, and yet are not, "slices of life." They are, more accurately, parables of life; and the social outcasts who people Harry Hope's "cheap gin-mill of the five-cent whiskey, last-resort variety" and the "cellar, resembling a cave," owned by Kostilev, are not, despite the naturalism of their portraiture, pictures of real men, but symbolic figures in a parable on man's fate. As such they are exceptionally well chosen; the "dregs of society," as the mark of extreme failure, are distress signals which urge inquiry into the nature of human disaster and the responsibility for it. Both plays are plays of dialogue rather than action, and what is done in them, reversing the usual method of drama, is an illustration of what is said. In each, a group of individuals, loosely bound together by a familiarity which breeds tolerant indifference and boredom and with enough in common to represent mankind by and large, is confronted by a solitary outsider who considers himself, and is considered by the group to be superior—to this extent, at least, that he is in a position to preach and to exhort them to a new way of life. In both plays this solitary individual is the repository of a "truth" unknown to the others, and in both, after a brief show of impressive authority, he leaves the scene of his activities in the same, or somewhat worse, condition than he had found it. Is the joke, then, on him? Are the tables turned? Is the prophet false, or at any rate, inadequate? And are the benighted souls whom he had tried to save in possession of a reality which his supposedly superior wisdom has not touched? Who, then, is better, and who is right? Who is to be blamed for the melancholy outcome of events, the prophet or those who refuse to become his disciples? The plays strike deep, deeper than their spoken arguments concerning the nature of truth and the value of illusion. Implicit in them are comparisons between theories of life and actual living, between idealism and reality: demands exacted by the mind and those made by the body, hope imposed by the spirit and the limits to hope set by the circumscribed potentialities of man; questions about the nature and the power of the will; and a search for an ethics that might be accepted as both just and possible in a human situation which is seen to be desperate. But here, with the kind of questions posed and the way they are examined, the similarities end. The answers given are amazingly different, and as one studies them one becomes aware that even the questions are not so similar as at first supposed.

Each play is constructed around a central character, and its meaning hinges on the interpretation of this man and of what he preaches, for he comes with a well-defined faith to correct his fellows; it is to him that they are constrained to respond individually and as a group, it is on him that thoughts and emotions converge. He is, in short, a test of moral principles, and the spectator must decide to what degree he should respect and trust him. In their natures, the two characters are entirely different. Gorky's Luke is a wanderer who, not from any newly found faith but from an accumulated store of sanctified dogma, hands out good advice wherever he happens to be to whoever will listen to him. He clucks sympathetically over men's complaints, tells little moral tales by way of illustrating his precepts, and, when the wretches he has been "saving" are drawn into a perilous situation and he himself is in danger of being caught and questioned by the authorities, slips out unperceived; for, with all his show of self-effacing, greathearted sympathy, he is not unmindful of his own safety—and he happens to be traveling without a passport. Hickey, on the other hand, enters with a program of reform, determined to make his friends happy, now that he himself has found happiness; and until the end, when he becomes a self-convicted felon, he has been a respected member of society. Nor is his scheme a ready-made concoction of untested, pious maxims; his recipe is drastic, and he has first tried it on himself. In the case of Hickey, there is no question of hypocrisy, but there is in the case of Luke.

When *The Lower Depths* was first performed in 1902, Luke was presented as a saintly character, and the play was interpreted as a lesson in brotherly love. That had not been Gorky's intention, as he himself explained in interviews at the time and in an article of 1933 in which—having described four types of "consolers," the sincere (an extremely rare variety), the professional, the vain, and finally "the most dangerous, clever, well-informed, and eloquent" of them all, the coldhearted men who cared about nothing so much as their own peace and comfort and consoled only because they could not be bothered with complaints—he declared that Luke belonged in the last division. "In our days," he added, "the consoler can be presented on the stage only as a negative and comic figure."

Gorky had intended Satin to be the real hero, but muffed the effect by leaving him off stage in some of the crucial moments of the play. Satin is in every respect at opposite poles from Luke, whom he appraises with his native acumen and honest incivility. "Pulp for the toothless" he calls him, but admits that in theory, at least, the wanderer has the right idea about man: namely, that man is large and free and must not be hampered. Satin, who sneers when he is sober and is eloquent when drunk, who is not apart from but very much of the group, on the spot when he is needed, sensible, and, above all, realistic in his understanding of what his fellowmen can and cannot do, has an undemonstrative, genuine sympathy which is infinitely more valuable than Luke's facile, soft-hearted, self-protecting kindliness: "You know how to do better than pity," Kleshch says to him, "you know how not to insult." And his rhetorical speech about man, which begins, "What is man? It is not you, not I, not they . . . no! It is you, I, they, the old man, Napoleon, Mahommed . . . all in one! Do you understand? It is—immense . . . ," is the culminating point of the play and the one that states its meaning. From Satin's standpoint Luke's pampering consolations, when they are not positively harmful—as in the case of the Actor, for whose suicide Satin holds the old man responsible—are insulting to man.

In *The Iceman Cometh* Satin's counterpart is Larry, "the only occupant of the room," according to the stage directions, "who is not asleep" when the curtain goes up, and who indeed remains terribly wide awake throughout the play, who speaks "sardonically," with "a comical intensity," considers himself aloof from all human affairs, "in the grandstand of philosophical detachment," but cannot help responding to the sufferings of "the breed of swine called men" with a sensitiveness and passion he would gladly suppress. He is discriminating and stern in his judgments and penetrating in his grasp of motives. He is not given to long pronouncements, does not try to influence men, but his influence is felt in what he is and in what he makes people do when they compel him to direct them; and, when he talks, it is with the aptness, wit, and brevity of poetry: "their ships will come in, loaded to the gunwales with cancelled regrets and promises fulfilled and clean slates and new leases"; "when man's soul isn't a sow's ear, it will be time enough to dream of silk purses"; and it is he who finds the right name for the Iceman, when he calls him the Iceman of Death. At the beginning of the play he makes a little speech that could be taken as the theme song of both *The Iceman Cometh* and *The Lower Depths*:

> What's it matter if the truth is that their favoring breeze has the stink of nickel whiskey on its breath, and their sea is a growler of lager and ale, and their ships are long since looted and scuttled and sunk on the bottom? To hell with the truth! As the history of the world proves, the truth has no bearing on anything. It's irrelevant and immaterial, as the lawyers say. The lie of a pipe dream is what gives life to the whole misbegotten mad lot of us, drunk or sober.

The "pipe dream" is the obvious leitmotif of *The Iceman Cometh,* as it is also that of *The Lower Depths,* the real theme of which, according to a splendid analysis by the Soviet critic Iury Iuzovsky,[3] is the question "What is Truth?" The characters of Gorky's play, this writer points out, are divided into well-marked groups with respect

[3] Iury Iuzovsky, *Dramaturgia Gor'kovo,* Chast' I (Moscow-Leningrad, 1940), pp. 61-161.

to the kind of truth they believe in: those, like the Actor, Pepel, Natasha, and Nastya, for whom illusion is truth; those, on the contrary, who believe only in the "truth of facts," like Bubnov, Kleshch, and the Baron, all of whom delight in pricking, variously, the bubble of man's hope—Bubnov with quiet satisfaction, Kleshch with bitterness, the Baron with a kind of sensual delight, "sneering out of envy," as Luke says of him; and, lastly, Luke and Satin who belong to neither category, and whose position Iuzovsky explains by a reference to Lenin's article, "What Is To Be Done?"—written in the same year as Gorky's drama. "One must day-dream," says Lenin in this article, and, quoting the nineteenth-century nihilist critic, Pisarev:

> My day-dream may be of such a kind as to catch up with the natural course of events, or it may go off completely at a tangent to where the natural course of events can never arrive. In the first instance, the day-dream does no harm; it may even strengthen and strengthen the energy of toiling mankind . . . In such day-dreams there is nothing that can prevent or paralyze the strength of workers . . . When there is a point of contact between the day-dream and life, then everything is going well . . .

comments that of the latter kind of day dream there is unfortunately too little in his time. *The Lower Depths,* says Iuzovsky, seems to give symbolic form to this distinction; Luke's is a day dream of slavery and leads to a dead end; Satin's is of freedom and opens a way out; the one goes off at a tangent, the other has contact with reality.

Nevertheless, whether they believe anything or not, the inhabitants of *The Lower Depths* retain, as individuals, a sense of their humanity and they suffer because of it; Circe has not deprived them of consciousness, and, even though they do not do very much, they retain the possibility of action. With the frequenters of Harry Hope's saloon the case is different. They are contented enough in their sodden stupor and are miserable only when, for a brief space, they are jerked into consciousness, for this robs their liquor of its potency to "paralyze." Once they are made to face themselves, the good-natured Americans, thrown into inward conflict by the sudden demonstration that their long-cherished beliefs about themselves are lies, become acrimonious and belligerent; the Russians, even the "romantic" ones, had been too sober and too unhappy from the start for any kind of pretense of mutual regard and general affability. In both plays, it would seem, amicable relations can exist only on the superficial basis of convenient indifference, the "live and let live" philosophy of those who have not chosen, but have been driven, to live together. The Russians have, indeed, much less sense of group solidarity than the Americans; all but wholly unaware of one another and much more callous, they appear to have theories about society but little capacity or desire for social living.

The real difference between the characters in the two plays, however, is not that of social relationships but of the kind of illusion they cherish and the nature of the "truth" they are invited to adopt. If both plays can be said to deal with illusion and reality, these terms have different meanings for their authors. "Truth" or "reality" for Gorky is not a metaphysical but a humanist concept; it involves not so much a recognition of that which is or may be, immutably, as of that which may or may not be done at a given moment. Freedom of will is here based simply on a practical view of possibilities. O'Neill's position is more sophisticated and complex; for him there is no distinction between useful and useless illusions, and no naive presentation of men as fully expressed by their beliefs. From an objective point of view, the "pipe dreams" here are all useless, but all are tragically inescapable and necessary to those who hold them; they are drawn not from the human consciousness of Circe's victims, nor from their idealistic hopes, but from painful, suppressed memories, the persistent iteration of recurrent images in troubled dreams. Here every man has been involved in something he wants to forget. Circe has helped him to oblivion, and the one real victory of his life is his capacity to forget. These men—all but one—unlike Gorky's, do not complain of the miserable state they are in. Parritt, the notable exception, commits suicide. The men of *The Lower Depths* are vaguely aware of some great solution to existence which they have not yet discovered, and the play exhorts them to seek a way that will lead them to discover it; those of *The Iceman Cometh* have no thought of anything beyond their individual well-being, which by now has been reduced to the form of drunken senselessness, and the play turns out to be a study of the impossibility of getting at the truth, indeed, a warning of the danger of going after it.

It is in keeping with this condition that the "leaders" differ as they do—that the American "prophet" is a salesman, peddling salvation as he peddles wash boilers, required to persuade a sales-resisting audience of the usefulness of his product, while the Russian is a wandering holy man, who preaches and consoles, leading despairing men who are only too ready to believe him along the path of human kindness, soothing them with assurances that their dreams are attainable. Both men are evil, Gorky's shrewdly and irresponsibly, O'Neill's, even in his noxiously commonplace sentimentality, rather pathetically and goodheartedly; for, whereas Luke's words are words only, Hickey is disastrously involved in what he preaches. Comically enough, neither accomplishes what he sets out to do—comically, because our sympathies are not with them. If the tone of the plays is on the whole tragic, the tragedy inheres not in the doom of the central characters but in the pathos of various episodes, and even more in implications, in what is not, rather than in what is, done or said. But if Luke and Hickey fail as prophets, it is not because they have misunderstood the values by which their audiences live—a passion for faith on the one hand, a desire for individualistic self-assertion on the other. Nor is it these premises, but something else, that is proved false in their failure.

What is at issue in Gorky's play is the relative usefulness—and *usefulness* is here the same as ultimate good—of two ideals: one, the Christian ideal of tender, pitying humility and inactive faith, the other, the materialist doctrine of forceful, self-reliant, practical action. In O'Neill's play the issue is the nature rather than the practicability of ideals. Social activity is the sphere of Gorky's thought, self-knowledge of O'Neill's. Though both are concerned with happiness, in *The Lower Depths* happiness is looked on as derivative, dependent on an intellectual grasp of values: let a man become conscious of his dignity and capacity, let him adopt an ideal which is possible for man, and he will realize it as an individual. In *The Iceman Cometh* happiness is seen to be immediate and primary; larger concepts may be valid only as abstract formulations of what men have done: let a man believe only what he has achieved—otherwise he will be ridiculous, self-deceived, and dangerous. The reason Luke fails is that he is neither serious nor honest in his relations with men; but Hickey fails because, in his desire to arouse Circe's victims to their original status as human beings with insight into themselves, he has attempted the impossible, for most of them cannot be roused, and those who can will kill themselves once they have understood what they are. Gorky's "message" is seriously meant as a program of conduct; O'Neill's is a poetic statement of disaster, presented only for the contemplation of those who care to look below the surface of human activity.

Murder is central to both plays; but in *The Lower Depths* it is accidental, based on passion, and is generally conceded to be regrettable, while in *The Iceman Cometh* it is more or less premeditated, rationalized to appear as an act of love, and is not a mere episode but the essence of the play. In fact, *The Iceman Cometh,* the latest of O'Neill's inquiries into the paradoxes of existence, is a prophecy of doom, of the willful and calculated murder by man of what he thinks he loves, a revelation of his unconscious hatreds and desire for death. Always concerned with illusion, O'Neill has presented it in many ways: in pictures of individuals pathetically or tragically frustrated because of some initial mistake they make about themselves or that others make about them, as in "Bound East for Cardiff," "Before Breakfast," "The Rope," *Beyond the Horizon, The Straw,* and *Diff'rent*; in symbols not of individuals but of man overwhelmed by the force of unconscious primitivism latent in him, as in *The Emperor Jones* and *The Hairy Ape*; in parables concerning the ethics of Western civilization, as in *The Fountain, Marco Millions,* and *Lazarus Laughed*; or in psychological probings of man's soul, as in *Desire Under the Elms, The Great God Brown, Strange Interlude,* and *Mourning Becomes Electra.* Despite great variation in focus and interest, certain factors remain constant enough throughout the plays to make O'Neill's work appear as a continuous philosophic investigation of the riddle of falsehood at the core of life, in the process of which several partial solutions have been reached, but no definitive one as yet. His plays are eerie with the ghosts of terrible dissatisfactions and of desperate guilt; and their darkness is hardly relieved by a hovering conviction that there is power in love and that an ultimate beneficent grandeur exists beyond the groping and raging consciousness of man, for it is in tragedy itself that men are shown to have attained their desires. Jones, in death, preserves the magnificent isolation he had wanted; Yank, in the brotherhood of monkeys, "belongs" at last; Ephraim Cabot's desolate farm is still "jimdandy"; Lavinia Mannon, who has dedicated herself to the punishment of a wrong, shuts herself away from life as the final phase of her life work—and so on. In an ironic way, death and suffering are always the price of attainment, while back of this human scene is "an infinite, insane energy which creates and destroys without other purpose than to pass eternity in avoiding thought," and is sometimes called God. A primitive, necessary, unthinking, intangible essence that insures perpetuity is shown to exist in opposition to the will of man, who desires extinction. "We're always desiring death for ourselves or others," says Nina Leeds. "Our lives are merely strange dark interludes in the eternal display of God the Father!"

The Iceman Cometh, perhaps more clearly than any of the other O'Neill plays, is a morality play, a variation on the ancient motif of the Dance of Death, with its modern, paradoxical twist of willed chance and desired catastrophe, where each man kills the thing he loves because he feels guilty of his inability to love enough. Harry Hope's saloon is Everywhere, and the men in it are drowning a secret guilt they cannot understand. Gorky's outcasts, on the other hand, are boldly, openly immoral; they admit the crimes they have committed and are not ashamed of them, for their crimes, being offenses not against themselves but against something hateful outside themselves, have, in a way, the aspect of righteous vengeance. The depths to which they have sunk are only social depths; what troubles them is a sense not of guilt but of inadequacy, and to find truth is their only salvation. But O'Neill seems to be saying that to live at all man must live on a lie, for the reward of truth is death. Gorky's man can live only by facing himself, O'Neill's cannot live if he faces himself.

The theme of O'Neill's play is not really the difference between illusion and reality, but the difference between two realities: one the reality of belief, the other the reality of the unrecognized and unacknowledgeable forces of existence. Between illusion and reality a man might choose, but O'Neill's two realities are not open to choice; they are related to each other in a fashion so tortuous as to elude consciousness. A man feels and believes the very opposite of what he thinks he feels and believes. And the reason for this is that the understandable necessity to live has imposed on him a habit of unconscious lying; he reiterates a faith in his will to live, in the great capacity and need of love which animates his life, whereas actually his desire is to die and the motivating force of his life is not love but hate. In short, the two realities which inform man's existence are so profoundly contradictory that consciousness must either pass them by, or deal with them in falsehoods, or obliterate itself. Man is, by definition, a deluded being. Thus the poor, harmless souls at Harry Hope's—good-natured, easy-going, and rather appealing with their vague beliefs in love and honor so long as they remain in their drunken stupor—exhibit, as soon as they are forced to consciousness, unsuspected, deep-seated, murderous hatreds. What Hickey's truth brings to light is that everything that seems good covers up basic evil: Hope, whose life of inactivity is postulated on the premise that he is mourning the death of Bessie whom he loved, suddenly finds himself calling her "that nagging bitch"; Jimmy Tomorrow, who thinks he has been drowning his sorrow at Marjorie's defection, admits, to his own surprise, that he never wanted her; Parritt is forced to acknowledge not only that he is guilty of virtual matricide but that this murder was caused by his hatred of his mother; and, as a piece of final irony, Hickey, in the very process of a touching disquisition on his lasting and passionate love of Evelyn, inadvertently blurts out: "You know what you can do with your pipe dream now, you damned bitch!"

In Gorky's view, what men need more than anything is a belief by which to steer their actions, but for O'Neill beliefs are irrelevant to both morality and happiness. Man is born guilty—O'Neill's attempt to rid himself of Puritanism seems to have brought him around to a metaphysical confirmation of its basic tenets—and the more he tries to clear himself of guilt the more entangled he becomes in it. For how shall the kind of truth which consciousness reveals be met except by death? What price life, O'Neill is asking, and is not genial enough to congratulate man on escaping destruction by the skin of his teeth; for, to his severe scrutiny of man, the death wish seems to have moral justification. The last of all illusions is that ideals are something other than Janus-faced inventions, distressing and comforting by turn, without reference to anything beyond themselves other than the reality of man's having to get through his life somehow. In earlier plays there had been a gentler note. "Do not wound me with wisdom," said the wise Kublai of *Marco Millions,* "Speak to my heart!" But now, how shall the heart be spoken to when it has forgotten the only language by which it can be addressed, when all poetic vision has been lost, the great unanalyzable substratum of experience has been given over to dissection, love and hate have become indistinguishable, and the pursuit of happiness has ended not in enjoyment but in oblivion? More unhappy than O'Neill's men, Gorky's are not so lost.

The essential difference in the two situations is perhaps best embodied in the real heroes of the plays: Satin, ruthless in his appraisal of individual failings but with a native respect for humanity and an ardent faith in its grandeur, and Larry, whose cynical philosophy is coupled with an instinctive sympathy of which he is ashamed, and whose sense of justice is based on a hopeless understanding of human beings. With these characters, it seems to me, their authors are identified: Gorky with the man of action, closely involved in the fate of his fellows, but more clear-eyed, farseeing, and confident than they, and able, therefore, to inspire them by a persuasive vision of their strength; O'Neill with the Grandstand Foolosopher, whose function it is to look unsquintingly on man's depravity and, when called upon, to discharge the unwelcome task not of judging men but of letting them pass judgment on themselves. The high point of Satin's act is a stirring speech on man, of Larry's, his waiting by the window to hear the sound of Parritt throwing himself from the fire escape (for Larry's finest deed is to free a man of guilt by driving him to suicide) —just as the purpose of Gorky's life was to stir men to action, and the function of O'Neill's has been to make them aware of the full meaning of the evil that is in them.

This contrast, to my mind, cannot be fully explained by the fact that O'Neill has long been preoccupied with Roman Catholicism, into which he was born, while Gorky was always an agnostic; for these titles of belief may point to tendencies of thinking and perceiving but can neither describe nor account for an artist's original view of life. Some might say that O'Neill's sophisticated, puritanical condemnation of man has proved to be a wise commentary on Gorky's naive Homeric pity, history having shown that it is better for men to mope in harmless inactivity than to follow a leader whose promises fail to take account of the nature of human motives, and that Circe's brutes had better be changed back to men before being urged to action. But to say this would be to disregard both the complexity of historical events and the kinds of plays we are here considering: one of them has as its aim to state a temporary ethical problem affecting men in an unsatisfactory society which might be changed; the other, to scrutinize the eternal dilemma of how conscious man is related to unconscious nature—aims so divergent as to make these two samples of Western art in the twentieth century almost as dissimilar as those produced by the cultures of Byzantium and of ancient Greece.

Notes on the Editor and Contributors

JOHN HENRY RALEIGH, Professor of English at the University of California, is the author of *Matthew Arnold and American Culture* and *The Plays of Eugene O'Neill.*

DORIS ALEXANDER is the author of *The Tempering of Eugene O'Neill* (1962), the first part of a scholarly biography. It covers O'Neill's life up to 1920.

BROOKS ATKINSON, now retired, was for many years drama critic for *The New York Times.* He is the author of many books on the theatre. During World War II he was a foreign correspondent.

ERIC BENTLEY, Brander Matthews Professor of Dramatic Literature at Columbia, is a translator, editor, and author, best known for his *The Playwright as Thinker, In Search of Theatre,* and *The Life of the Drama.*

CROSWELL BOWEN, journalist and free-lance writer, is the author of the first full-length biography of O'Neill, *Curse of the Misbegotten.*

ROBERT BRUSTEIN, Dean of the Yale School of Drama, has been drama critic for the *New Republic* since 1959 and is the author of *The Theatre of Revolt.*

BARRETT H. CLARK (1890-1953), was a playwright, author, and editor, best known for his editions of *America's Best Plays.* His *Eugene O'Neill,* originally published in 1926, was the first book on the subject.

CYRUS DAY, Professor of English at the University of Delaware, has published *English Song Books, 1651-1702* and *Songs of John Dryden.*

DORIS FALK, Professor of English at Douglas College, Rutgers University, is the author of *Eugene O'Neill and the Tragic Tension.*

ARTHUR GELB is a magazine writer and has been associated in various capacities with *The New York Times* since 1944. His wife, Barbara, is a free-lance writer. Together they collaborated on *O'Neill,* the most comprehensive biography of the playwright yet written.

ROSAMOND GILDER was associated with *Theatre Arts Monthly* from 1924-1949. She has been involved with many national and international theatre endeavors and is the author of *Enter the Actress, John Gielgud's Hamlet,* and other books.

LAWRENCE LANGNER is an inventor and a man of the theatre, having been a playwright, an author, and the founder of the Theatre Guild. He tells his own story in *The Magic Curtain,* an autobiography.

MARY MCCARTHY, drama critic, social critic, literary critic, and novelist, was from 1937 to 1957 drama critic for the *Partisan Review*. *Sights and Spectacles* is a collection of her reviews. Miss McCarthy is best known for *The Group, The Man in the Brooks Brothers Suit,* and other novels and short stories.

HELEN MUCHNIC is Professor of Russian at Smith College and the author of *Dostoevsky's English Reputation* and *From Gorky to Pasternak*. She is a frequent contributor to the New York *Review of Books*.

GEORGE JEAN NATHAN (1882-1958), the celebrated drama critic, was co-editor and co-founder of the *American Mercury* with H. L. Mencken. A personal friend of O'Neill, he wrote about him as a man and a dramatist on many occasions. Nathan was the author of numerous books on a wide range of subjects.

KARL SCHRIFTGRIESSER was a feature writer for *The New York Times* in the 1940's.

JOHN S. WILSON was the drama critic for the now defunct newspaper *PM* in the 1940's.

SOPHUS WINTHER, Professor of English at the University of Washington, is a novelist and critic. He is the author of *Eugene O'Neill* (first edition 1934; revised and enlarged in 1961).

S. J. WOOLF was an artist-writer for *The New York Times* in the 1940's. The report of his interview with O'Neill was accompanied by a sketch of the subject.

Chronology of Important Dates

[Note: It is impossible to date the exact beginning of any of the great technological inventions that for the last century or more have been steadily transforming human life. But it is important to note that O'Neill was born in the age of the gaslight and the horsedrawn carriage, with the train being the only fast mode of transportation, and America isolated from the rest of the world. He lived to see, or hear of, atom bombs, rockets, and the "Cold War."]

	O'Neill	*Other Events*
1888	October 16: Born in New York City.	
1898		Spanish-American War.
1912	December 24: Entered a TB sanitarium where he decided to become a playwright (released, as arrested case, Spring, 1913).	Death of Strindberg [the playwright O'Neill most admired]; English translation of Strindberg's *Dance of Death*; a great deal of ferment, creativity, and high hopes for the arts in America.
1914	Spring: Composed *Bound East for Cardiff*, his first play to be produced.	Beginning of World War I.
1915		Founding of the Washington Square Players and the Provincetown Players, both noncommercial "little" theatre groups.
1916	Summer: *Bound East for Cardiff* produced by Provincetown Players.	
1918		End of World War I.
1919		The Washington Square Players become the Theatre Guild, producers of most of O'Neill's plays.

	O'Neill	*Other Events*
1920	February 2: New York production of *Beyond the Horizon.* June: Awarded Pulitzer Prize for *Beyond the Horizon.*	
1922	May: Awarded Pulitzer Prize for *Anna Christie.*	
1928	February: Left for three years in Europe; the real beginning of his life of exile and isolation. May: Awarded Pulitzer Prize for *Strange Interlude.*	
1929	July 22: Married Carlotta Monterey (his third marriage).	The beginning of the Great Depression.
1936	November 12: Awarded Nobel Prize for Literature.	
1939	June 8-November 26: Wrote *The Iceman Cometh* at Tao House, Danville, California.	Beginning of World War II.
1945		July 16: Explosion of first atomic bomb; end of World War II.
1953	November 27: Died in Boston. December 2: Interred in Forest Hills Cemetery, Boston.	
1956	February: Stockholm production of *Long Day's Journey Into Night.* May: Second New York production of *The Iceman Cometh.* November: New York production of *Long Day's Journey Into Night.*	
1957	Fourth Pulitzer Prize for *Long Day's Journey Into Night.*	

1977

Books by Walter D. Edmonds

ROME HAUL

THE BIG BARN

ERIE WATER

MOSTLY CANALLERS

DRUMS ALONG THE MOHAWK

CHAD HANNA

YOUNG AMES

IN THE HANDS OF THE SENECAS

THE WEDDING JOURNEY

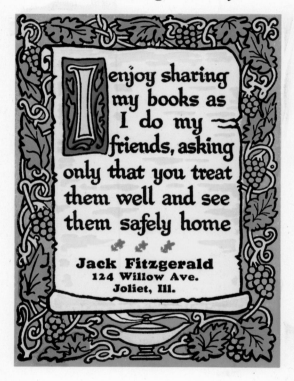

I enjoy sharing my books as I do my friends, asking only that you treat them well and see them safely home

Jack Fitzgerald
124 Willow Ave.
Joliet, Ill.

THE
Wedding Journey

WALTER D. EDMONDS

DRAWINGS BY ALAN TOMPKINS

AN ATLANTIC MONTHLY PRESS BOOK

LITTLE, BROWN AND COMPANY · BOSTON

1947

FIRST EDITION

Published October 1947

LC# 47-5530

ATLANTIC—LITTLE, BROWN BOOKS
ARE PUBLISHED BY
LITTLE, BROWN AND COMPANY
IN ASSOCIATION WITH
THE ATLANTIC MONTHLY PRESS

Published simultaneously
in Canada by McClelland and Stewart Limited

PRINTED IN THE UNITED STATES OF AMERICA

TO
KAY *and* HENRY BRAGDON
Who were born closer
to the old canal than I

I

*S*HE had often heard her mother say that freeing Negroes made them impudent, and for a moment she thought that the packet-boat stewardess was going to be distressingly impertinent. When she asked her name, the black girl replied, "Viney, miss," and then asked, as if she were hostess on the boat instead of merely a hired servant, "An' what's yo' name, miss?"

Bella, who had been Bella Vincent only six short hours ago, felt her cheeks grow pink. She tried to look at Viney coolly and to make her voice sound matter-of-fact; but when the words came out they were quick, almost hushed.

"I'm Mrs. Willcox."

There it was. She had often said it to herself —"Mrs. Willcox"—but now it was a fact before the world. The marriage ceremony, her father reading the service, the flowers on the altar and the flowers round her veil, her mother sniffing softly, and her sister Clorinda behind her, the music, even Roger, putting the ring on her finger —all those things seemed parts of the properly ordered climax of her maidenhood. But now that she had said to this pert-looking Negro girl, "I'm Mrs. Willcox," she knew that she was married.

Viney's bright eyes regarded her so knowingly that she had a sudden impulse to run out of the cabin and find Roger. But she needed sprucing after the dusty stage ride from Albany to the Schenectady dock; she wanted to look her best at supper that evening; and inside of her she felt that somehow it was important to the success of her marriage to assert herself before this girl.

Viney, fingering the white apron that neatly covered her red dress, bobbed her bandannaed head and curtsied unexpectedly. Then, as she raised her black face again, her limber mouth opened and she showed all her teeth in a beaming smile.

"You jes' married, Mis' Willcox?"

Bella nodded, blushing again.

"Lawsy!" Viney breathed. "'Tain't often I got a bran'-new honeymoon lady to look after. I trust yo' trip will be pleasurable, Mis' Willcox."

She bent down for the bags with a submissive droop of her shoulders, and Bella realized that she wasn't impudent after all. She was only trying to be friendly.

"Which bed you like the bes', Mis' Willcox?"

Bella glanced round the ladies' cabin. She had never been on a canal packet before, and it looked very strange to her. In spite of the white paneling and the bright red curtains at the windows,

the red-clothed table and the brass-shaded lamp,
the room seemed small and bald. The beds were
stanchions hinged from the walls; canvas was
laced across the iron frame, and resting on it was
the thinnest conceivable mattress.

"There's only two other ladies," Viney said.
"They ain't got here yet, so you can have yo' pick,
Mis' Willcox."

Bella said, "Maybe that one in the front."

Viney started to move towards it. Then she
halted, still holding on to the bags, and said tactfully, "That sure is the quietest. But you don't
get so good air, and the nights they been hot
lately, mis'."

"Perhaps you're right, Viney. Which one would
you recommend?"

Viney pursed her lips.

"Well, if I was a lady making selection of these
beds, mis', I'd declare for this one in the corner.
I reckon I'd get mo' air. And though it's right
next the saloon wall and I'd hear the gentlemen
playing ca'ds, it's mos' apt I'd hear them any-
ways. It's nice to have a corner bed too, with
walls to yo' head. And then you'd have me handy
to call me if you want me in the night."

"Where do you sleep, Viney?"

Viney giggled.

"Don' get much sleep sometimes, but I got a
pallet on the floor there." She indicated the floor
beside the door to the main saloon.

"I think I'll take the corner bed, then," Bella said with definiteness. Viney nodded. She laid Bella's bags against the wall and asked whether she should open them.

"You can open the big one, Viney."

"Does yo' want to change?"

Bella hesitated. She would like to go right out to Roger, but the prospect of fresh clothes was enticing.

"Yes," she said. "I'd like the green dress."

Viney said, "If you like to wash yo'self, I'll show you where."

Bella nodded, and Viney conducted her to the door in the far corner, where, in a little closet, she found pitcher and basin and soap. Taking

her own towel and brush and comb, she rubbed off the dry sandy dust that seemed to have coated her from head to foot. She did up her hair again, using the green net that matched her dress, and studied herself in the small glass.

It was a very young face that looked back at her: a small straight nose, a small pointed chin. Only the warm brown eyes with their straight, rather heavy black brows and curling lashes, and the wide mobile mouth, the upper lip so short it seemed to tremble on the verge of smiling, kept it from being insignificant. It was an eager face, so live it seemed to shy at life, and almost naïvely honest.

But it did not satisfy her at all. She wished it could have been blond and beautiful like her sister's: Clorinda was the kind of girl that people looked at. As Aunt Francine had often said, "There's nothing statuesque about Bella." All the family had expected, when Roger first came to call, that he had his eye on Clorinda. Even Clorinda hadn't troubled to deny it. The fact that it was now Bella who found herself in the ladies' washroom on the *Western Lion* bound for Buffalo and Ohio, the wife of Roger Willcox, seemed utterly, delightfully incredible.

As she pulled out her curls before her ears, Bella found that she was smiling back at the face in the glass. "Red as a garden radish," she whispered.

5

Then, just outside the window, she heard a man's feet walking up and down the passenger dock. As she recognized the step, rather deliberate, a little heavy, the walk of a big man, her flush waved deeper. Roger was waiting for her. She had married him that morning. She would never forget today with its warm high clouds sailing loftily—August 18, 1835. But she forgot the final pat for her hair. Leaving the towel and brush and comb lying whichway for the colored girl to pick up, she rushed out into the cabin.

Viney was exclaiming softly over the green dress.

"Quick," said Bella. "Oh, quick, Viney."

She slipped out of her traveling dress and held up her arms. She stood for an instant that way in her shift, with the striped sunlight from the shutters marking her, slim and still and white. With a hushed murmuring sound, the Negro girl passed the green dress over Bella's arms and patted it down. Bella's fingers flew over the laces.

"Give me my bonnet, Viney. And the blue scarf."

She was gone through the door.

Viney, slowly folding the traveling dress, listened to the rapid tap of Bella's feet traversing the saloon, running up the steps to the deck, and suddenly turning demure.

"Lawsy!" she breathed.

II

*B*ELLA came out into the bright glare on deck and glanced over the passenger dock, looking for Roger. When her eyes found him, her heart gave a little jump. He was standing with his back to her, talking to an elderly man. But Bella did not look at the stranger. At sight of Roger's broad shoulders filling his blue coat, the buff trousers fitting his narrow hips and straight legs so perfectly, the close-cut, curly black hair just showing under the brim of his hat, she felt suddenly shy.

His back was to her, but she knew exactly how his hands were folded on the head of his stick; she knew that the right wing of his stock was a little too long; she could tell from the bend of his head that he was smiling politely. But seeing him so, talking to an utter stranger, it came over her that she did not know Roger at all. And she was on a canal packet, a public conveyance. There was no familiar atmosphere of family life for her to retreat into now.

When Roger had stepped into her father's study to tell him their news, she had gone upstairs to find her mother. Her mother was sewing in a corner of the sitting room, where she had her table and a view down Hawk Street, and when Bella had come in she had said, "Good gracious, Bella! What is it?" And on Bella's telling her she had been very much surprised. "Of course Mr. Willcox comes of very good stock, but his family have been west for so many years now, I hardly feel I know them any more. I'm sure he's a worthy young man. His manners are good, certainly. Your father will know." She always took refuge from responsibility in her husband's opinions.

But Clorinda had been even more surprised. "Don't tease, Bella!" she had exclaimed. There had been spots of red in her cheeks; she had looked almost hectic; but as soon as she had been convinced she had said, "Your brats will be blacker than Portuguese."

The wind pushed Bella's skirts against her knees, and she found that she was flushing again; she wished she could conquer that ridiculous weakness; but it had been a stupid thing for Clorinda to say, even if she were piqued.

A blaring horn almost deafened her right ear. "Don't worry, ma'am. That's only a freight boat."

One of the *Western Lion's* crew was standing beside her on the steering deck. She glanced at his weather-lined hard face and found him smiling. He was pointing to the other side of the basin, where a thin pair of mules bowed down against their collars. The driver walked behind them; his blue shirt was open to the sun and wind all the way down to his belt, so that she could see his chest naked and furred. He was swinging a heavy long-lashed whip with a short stock. While Bella watched he cut the nearest mule across the withers, leaving a black welt. The beast clamped back its ears. She saw it shudder from the stroke.

The boat came by at the end of the hundred-foot towrope. Its square bow, the paint yellow and faded, thrust heavily against the ripple. A woman was cramming her arms with wash from a line stretched over the pit. The wind tugged her skirt back between her legs, molding them so close that Bella saw she wore no underthings. The steersman, hip against the rudder stick, yelled to the woman as he lifted his horn to his lips. His cheeks filled and emptied, and the blare again was deafening. The woman nodded her head sullenly to what he had told her and stepped out in her bare feet on the catwalk. The wash made a red and white puff under her face, like a bunch of preposterous flowers; and, as their eyes met, Bella saw with astonishment that the woman could not be more than eighteen years old and that, in a rough way, she was handsome. The girl managed to toss her chin above the wash, but when she turned in front of the steersman he struck her shoulder with his fist, spat over the side, wiped his mouth, and grinned at Bella.

"Rough, tough, and nasty," the packet-boat hand at her side said scornfully.

She did not answer him, but turned quickly to go to Roger. She felt frightened and upset and close to tears; she wanted to be near, to touch someone she knew. She had never seen a woman struck before.

Roger was walking back along the dock beside the elderly gentleman, his head slightly bowed to catch the other's words. He looked so calm, he walked so almost solemnly—the way he looked when he first walked into the house on Eagle Street—that she was glad he was not actually too handsome. "But he *is* handsome," she said to herself. "Clorinda thought so." And her heart gave a little bounce as she moved towards the plank, steadying her skirts with both hands. She felt as sure as anyone could be that Roger would never strike her.

She looked up for an instant as she stepped on the plank and caught his eye. His face had a high, even color, his mouth was composed and serious, but his eyes crinkled slightly at the corners. He looked amused at something; she wondered uneasily whether he could read her thoughts.

She ran down the plank to the dock and found herself meeting the admiring gaze of the elderly gentleman.

"Bella, this is Mr. Atterbury. He's making the trip west to Buffalo on our boat. Mr. Atterbury, this is my wife."

Roger looked prodigiously tall and strong, and Bella felt an almost suffocating pride in him. She curtsied formally to Mr. Atterbury, but she could hardly take her eyes off Roger in time to avoid an impoliteness.

Mr. Atterbury had removed his hat and laid it gently against his waistcoat. He was dressed quietly and elegantly in a black coat that seemed, however, a little travel-worn. His face she thought gentlemanly, with a narrow chiseled nose and a pleasant mouth under a white mustache; and he had waving white hair.

"It isn't often, I assure you, Mrs. Willcox, that an old traveler like myself faces a long journey lightened by the prospect of such delightful company."

He sounded almost old-fashioned to her, and his bow was low. Glancing out of the corner of her eye, Bella saw Roger wasn't looking at either of them; he had a fixed look in his eye that she had noticed once when Mrs. Vincent had invited their Albany relations to meet him. Guiltily she realized that she must have seemed a long time in the ladies' cabin to Roger. But she gave Mr. Atterbury a smile and her glove to touch and said that she also anticipated a delightful trip.

As he smiled to them both she saw how bright

13

his blue eyes were and thought that before his hair turned it must have been very fair.

Mr. Atterbury was saying, "Couldn't we sit together at supper, we three?"

Bella felt her hand drawn under Roger's arm. He said, "Yes. That would be splendid," and bowed stiffly.

Mr. Atterbury handed his satchel to the boat-man and followed him aboard.

III

*D*ARLING," Roger said quietly, "you're perfectly lovely."

Bella allowed her fingers to press his forearm and felt them hugged tight against his ribs. She was sure she could feel his ribs through the coat and she thought she could also feel his heart thumping inside.

He was walking her down the dock, his free hand holding his watch out of the fob pocket.

"We'll be starting in ten minutes," he said aloud for the benefit of some dock loafers. "It doesn't look as if we'd have many passengers."

But as soon as they were out of earshot his voice filled and he bent over close to her ear.

"Do you think you can stand it, dear?"

"What, Roger?"

"Being cooped up on that boat four whole days?"

She looked up at him, startled by the baffled note in his voice. For an instant his eyes seemed too close to bear. Her knees went weak under her and she had to hold hard on his arm, feeling herself enveloped by his impatience until she was almost sick. She caught the toe of her shoe in the hem of the green dress, and felt him lift and steady her. The warm wind blew in her face, her head cleared, and she thought, "He's never seen this dress and hasn't even noticed it yet." But he had told her she was lovely, and she had seen that he thought she was beautiful, and that seemed so wonderful that nothing else mattered. For Clorinda had always been the beauty of the family—it had always been spoken of at home. And then Bella realized that the things taken for granted at home had no more standing for her in the world. There were just she and Roger. There were no comforting retreats left to her. Nothing except the ladies' cabin of the *Western Lion*. She did not know what she thought about that; she did not know what to say.

She didn't have to answer.

Roger said abruptly: "It's always hard waiting for a boat to start."

He had stopped her at the end of the packet dock and was looking up the canal, his broad chin set and a thin crease between his eyes. His arm was solid under her hand, he stood very straight, and she realized gratefully that he wasn't asking her to answer. It was almost as if he understood.

Her pride returned and she lifted her chin as she stood at his side, so that they looked west together. They could see all the town that lay west of them, the brick houses with their gardens to the river and the smoke from their chimneys climbing against the late afternoon sky; and, leading straight away along the southern bank of the river, the canal, boats moving on it here and there, the mules in the distance like teams of ants harnessed by spider threads to chips; and then the green country, and the hills rolling gently to right and left, gathering a blue haze in their valleys.

A bugle sounded, and they wheeled hurriedly to find that behind their backs the boat had come to life. The captain was stepping decisively out from the passenger agent's box; two women and three men were crowding up the plank to the deck; and a couple of men had taken hold of the tie ropes, holding them in their hands, their heads turned towards the steersman. A quick thump of hoofs sounded across the dock, and a pair of horses, hitched tandem, came out of the street and took a stand a little ahead of the bow. A handler hooked the singletree to the towrope, and a driver boy, like a red-jacketed, active little monkey, scrambled up to his saddle on the rear horse. The captain cast his eye over everything. He was standing on the top deck, bugle in hand.

"*Aboard!*" he shouted.

He lifted his bugle to his lips.

Bella felt Roger almost swing her off her feet. "Come on," he said.

She had no idea that they had come so far from

17

the boat. They would have to run. Roger tightened his grip on her arm. He was half carrying her. She stole a look up at him, knowing she could not fall while he held her. All the baffled helplessness was gone from his face. He turned his head suddenly and gave her a whole-souled grin.

"Run, Bella," he said. "I don't think our bags would have much fun without us, even at Niagara Falls."

Under her skirts Bella's feet ran smoothly to match his long stride. The wind rocked her skirt under her from side to side, so that she seemed to skim over the rough planking. Her face was bright and hot as she caught the captain's hand, to be steadied up the gangplank.

The captain was smiling at her, the steersman was smiling at her; so were the passengers who had arrived late.

Roger handed her up to the deck that made a roof for the saloon and helped her arrange her scarf.

"We're off," he said. "Four days, darling. Then we'll go out to Niagara and have a week to ourselves, just you and me."

"And the bags," Bella said demurely.

"You're baggage enough for me," he said.

She turned very pink on discovering that the captain had come up to them and was listening tolerantly to everything they said. He wheeled to wave his arm at the passenger agent. "Got the time?" he bawled. "Write it down." He walked to the edge of the deck and shouted to the two men, forty feet away, to cast off the ropes. You could see that the captain knew his importance.

He looked over his shoulder at Roger and said, "Four days? Well, I'll give you a run for your money, mister. Maybe I'll shade it under four days. It's a light trip and we're out to bust time wide open. The company's given me a hundred dollars to pay my fines for speeding."

"If you do it under four days I'll buy you a parcel of the finest segars in Buffalo," Roger said; and the captain laughed at them.

"Don't worry, mister. I've had couples like you on this packet before, and though I never figured out why they was in such a lather to get a look at Niagara Falls, I always got them there on time."

He slapped the end of the bugle to his mouth, and the notes rang over the town. Dock-wallopers stopped wrestling with bales and barrels to see the *Western Lion* start; Red Bird packets were fliers, and knew how to start in style. They cheered as the team took up the slack. The driver boy shrilled profanely at his horses and swung his whip.

"Feed it to them, boy," the captain roared. "Pump it in."

The calks of the team's shoes ripped splinters from the planks. They shook up a trot. Under her feet Bella felt a tremor from their tugs. A ripple forked from the stern, jellying the reflections against the dock piles. Well ahead, a freight boat, hauling out of town, swung into midstream; their team stopped to let the rope lie on the towpath, and the packet team and packet boat passed over it while the freight crew looked on.

When they were past, Bella turned to watch the freight boat take up its way. The driver's whip made pops of sound like the champagne corks at her wedding breakfast.

"Feeling homesick?" Roger asked.

"No," said Bella honestly. It was only Schenectady she was leaving, the quaint brick houses,
the crowded canal basin, and the great bridge—
she had heard her father say it was the greatest
bridge in all America. It was the first landmark
on her journey, and, leaving it behind, she felt
the world unfolding for her as the water unfolded
for the packet's bow.

IV

*M*R. NEILSON said, "I do not know whether you hold prayers on your boat at night, Captain Harrow, but if you would like them, or if the company would like them, I should be only too glad to oblige."

Mr. Neilson was a minister returning to Rochester after a month's sojourn at Ballston Spa. He explained that his devoted congregation insisted on his going there every summer to recuperate after the winter's preaching. His heart was none too strong. This amused Bella and Roger and Mr. Atterbury, because, in addition to the brandy served with the water, Mr. Neilson had ordered himself a bottle of Old London port wine. He was an amply nourished individual in faultless clericals, and his wife seated herself where everyone could see the diamonds on her left hand. The entire company appeared relieved when the captain said, "Thank you, Mr. Neilson, but I'll leave it to the passengers."

Bella had a vague feeling that, if Mr. Neilson had been her father, instead of asking the captain he would have started prayers promptly at nine o'clock.

The steward cleared the table of dessert plates, and Mr. Atterbury ordered an apricot cordial for the three of them. Sipping the unaccustomed drink, Bella glanced round the saloon. It was wonderful to think that while they were eating this comfortable meal the boat was passing the riverside meadows at better than four miles an hour.

There was a pleasant coolness, and a faint fresh smell of grass under dew in the air fluttering the curtains. But the lamp slung over the table burned without flickering. There was no sound of travel, no rattle of trace links, no squeak of springs, no rumble of wheels. There was no sound at all but the roar of bullfrogs among lily pads in the set-backs, and since sunset that had been continual. Only when the driver boy's voice came back to them shrilly crying, "Bridge!" and the steersman answered, "Low bridge!" were the passengers aware that every minute saw them further west.

The supper had been pleasant; the company was a quiet one. Mrs. Neilson, indeed, described in intimate detail her very large acquaintance-ship, all of whom appeared to be either wealthy or distinguished, but as soon as she had listed them she seemed to regard her social duty to the company as performed for the evening. The talk clung mildly to the weather, the crops, the growing tightness of credit, the animosity of President Jackson for Nicholas Biddle and the United States Bank, and the low price of pork. On this last subject they listened to the determined views of the traveler for the Troy Nail Works, who delivered his theories with punches as emphatic as one of his factory's stamping engines. He was a small, spry man, wearing soiled clothes and an opulent watch fob, who had introduced himself as L. D. Jones. At supper he laid his half-smoked segar beside his plate—otherwise he kept it in the handiest corner of his mouth.

Besides Mr. L. D. Jones, the passenger list included the Willcoxes, Mr. Atterbury and the Neilsons, a Mr. Jason who was noncommittal about some properties in Illinois, and a Mrs. Cashdollar, a widow, who lived in Utica.

To Bella they seemed kind but dull. She could not help contrasting their appearance with Roger's or their conversation with Mr. Atterbury's.

Mr. Atterbury had had a career, and during supper he touched on it from time to time. Bella could not have said what his business consisted of, but it had apparently carried him all over the country. He seemed to know the best people in every state in the Union, from New Orleans to Boston, Massachusetts. He had traveled in every sort of conveyance, public and private—on steamboats, in sailing vessels, by horseback, alone, through the wildest parts of the continent. He had been on a flatboat going down the Ohio and had a brush with the river pirates; he had been held up by a highwayman on the Cumberland Road and got away not only with his life but with his money. He told his adventures with a light touch, his voice gentle, leaving to Bella's and Roger's imagination the more dramatic parts. He did not need to boast; the bare recital on that peaceful boat, his quiet face, his white hair, served his story well.

As she gazed round the saloon, making her eyes familiar with the order of packet-boat living —from the folded bed stanchions, which the men would sleep on, to the kitchen door and the small library with its settee and bull's-eye windows under the steersman's deck—Bella felt excited and gay. Her dark eyes were bright, her red lips curved, and when she laughed at something Mr. Atterbury said her laughter had a lilt that made even Mr. Neilson glance up from his contemplation of Old London. She did not mind the men's glances. She could see from the corner of her eye that Roger was proud of her. Her heart warmed with friendliness for all of them. She did not even mind Mrs. Neilson's veiled conveyance of hostility, or Mrs. Cashdollar's obvious amusement. She hardly noticed the two women. She was in Roger's hands, and as long as he liked her she felt her spirits winged.

V

*T*HE BOAT slid along peacefully. Only Mr.
L. D. Jones remained at table: his pot hat on the
back of his head, the segar lifeless in the corner
of his mouth, his order books spread out around
him.

Mr. and Mrs. Neilson had disposed themselves
in the library in such a manner that the entrance
of anyone else would have seemed impertinent.
Mr. Jason had taken a newspaper to the chair
under the lamp beside the stairs, and Mrs. Cashdollar had retired to the ladies' cabin, where her
rather heavy voice could be heard in conversation with Viney.

Bella listened to Mr. Atterbury with counter-
feit attentiveness. She felt Roger's glance upon
her profile and she was thinking, with the monotonous tick of the saloon clock in her ears, that
Clorinda would by now have eluded her mother's
discussion of the wedding; she would have gone
up to the room they used to share and begun her
careful preparations for bed. And here was she,
Bella, traveling with Roger, among strangers,
farther west already than any of her family had

26

ever been. She smiled to herself, thinking of Clorinda, but not unkindly, for Clorinda had lost.

Mr. Atterbury, seeing the smile, glanced casually at Roger, smiled himself, and brought his anecdote skillfully to a sudden ending. He rose from the bench and stepped across to one of the windows.

"It's a beautiful warm evening," he said. "I should think you two might like a turn on deck."

Roger met Bella's eyes.

"Do you think it will be damp?" he asked in his serious voice. "My wife is very sensitive to damp."

She almost sputtered, but caught herself in time. He sat so solemn, he so nearly managed to look stodgy, that for an instant he had taken her in. In Albany she would never have suspected Roger of being capable of such deceit. They were only a few hours west of Schenectady, too, and she wondered, "What will he be like when we reach Buffalo?" But she almost gurgled when Mr. Atterbury put his hand through the open window and said, "There's quite a heavy dew, Mr. Willcox. You had better take cloaks for your wife."

Nobody in the saloon seemed to be listening to them, but as she passed the table on her way to the ladies' cabin she saw Mr. L. D. Jones, obviously thinking he was not observed, look up from his books and wink across his dead segar at Mr. Jason.

The lamp was low in the ladies' cabin. Mrs. Cashdollar was propped up on her bed with a glass balanced on her ample stomach, and there was an unmistakable odor of whiskey. Viney stood at her side, holding a pitcher of fresh water.

At Bella's entrance they both looked round, Viney with a properly expressionless face, Mrs. Cashdollar with a broad smile.

"Going on deck, dearie?" Mrs. Cashdollar asked. "It's hot enough."

Bella said, "Yes," stiffly.

She did not like Mrs. Cashdollar. The woman did not look quite proper.

"I should think your boy was getting pretty impatient. It's hard luck having a honeymoon on a packet boat."

Bella said, "Viney, please give me my cape."

"Ain't it there by the bed?" asked Mrs. Cashdollar.

"I suppose it is," said Bella. "I asked Viney to give it to me."

Mrs. Cashdollar took the pitcher from the Negress and said good-humoredly, "Go ahead, girlie."

"Yes, Mis' Cashdollah. Yes, Mis' Willcox."

Viney fetched the cloak.

Mrs. Cashdollar regarded Bella's flushed face with a friendly glance.

"Dearie," she said, "you don't like me because

you've never seen anybody like me before. But I like you. If you'll take a suggestion, you'll get on to the bow deck and sit against the wall. I thought of that when I picked this bow bed. You can sit there and I'll keep that Neilson cat from having Viney open the window, and you can kiss all you want to and nobody'll hear you."

Bella flushed furiously.

"Don't get mad. You don't have to. But take a little pity on your boy, dearie. And if you want blankets, just tap on the window and I'll have Viney pass them out."

Accepting her cloak, Bella said, "Thank you," very formally, and went out.

VI

*R*OGER was waiting for her at the saloon
steps. Mr. Atterbury was hunting in his bag for
a segar. None of the others appeared to notice
them, so Bella slipped across to Roger and took
his arm and they went on deck.

There they found the night and the country,
and the steersman leaning idly on the rudder
stick while the banks slipped past him.

"Evening, ma'am and sir," he said quietly. "It's
clear tonight."

"Good evening," Roger said.

"Good evening," said Bella.

Her heart filled with the quiet and the coolness and the warm firm touch of Roger's arm
under her fingers. She drew her skirts over her
knees and climbed the short flight to the top deck
with him. From there they looked out over the
towpath.

The moon had not yet risen, but a mist lay on
the Mohawk, and there was starlight on the
mist. They were passing a long riverside pasture,
so narrow that the sound of the water against the
riverbanks was audible. A herd of cows grazed

below the towpath. Now and then, when one lifted her head, they heard a bell clank gently.

The pressure of Roger's arm drew Bella forward. The driving lantern on the bow standard shed a yellow luminance against the canal bank, showing them the reeds and the grass slipping backward, and rocking lily pads with their stiff blooms like golden goblets. The air was damp against their faces and carried here a scent of ferns. From the tow cleat, twelve feet back on the right side of the boat, the towrope curved up towards the towpath like a silver cord.

Bella pressed herself against Roger's side as they stood together. His arm jerked suddenly from hers and stole round under the cape, round her waist, enfolding her, until she felt herself enveloped. She felt herself in darkness under her cape, as if it were a private world, and he had entered it.

He said softly, "Four days. There isn't a corner where someone can't see you."

His arm shook. She was quite still; she felt poised, so light that if a wind had come upon her suddenly only his arm would have held her to the boat.

"Roger," she whispered, "couldn't we go down on that front deck and sit with our backs against the ladies' cabin?"

"It's right in the light," he said.

"I know, Roger, but the steersman couldn't see

33

us. And Mrs. Cashdollar said she would pass out blankets if we tapped on the window."

"Mrs. Neilson would hear us."

"Mrs. Cashdollar promised to keep her from opening the bow windows."

"Bless her, you darling."

Forward in the darkness out along the towpath, the driver boy's voice cried, "Bridge!"

Suddenly they heard the team's hoofs trotting; then the silence swallowed the hoofbeats.

"Low bridge!" the steersman called behind them. The towrope was disappearing into blackness. The timbers of the bridge loomed.

"Hey, mister. Down!"

Roger jumped from the saloon deck on to the forward deck. He turned in the light of the lantern and held up his arms.

"Quick," he said.

Bella felt her heart spring in her breast as she met his eyes. The cape fluttered behind her; his hands caught her and she was against his chest; and her cape flew forward like wings about them both. She lifted her face and his lips came down on hers.

Roger let her go, and for the first time her feet came against the deck. But she stood still inside her cloak, with no breath in her, and her mouth still raised and her eyes closed.

He laughed softly and kissed her eyes.

On the rear deck the steersman was glancing

out at the far bank and whistling "Red River Girl." They stepped from each other and looked round. Two warm blankets lay under the window, and pinned to one of them by a hairpin was a piece of paper bearing in an illiterate scrawl: "I heard the old cat coming in and passed them out for you."

They read it, laughing softly together.

"Do you know what she does, Bella?"

"No."

"Captain Harrow says she runs a cook's agency for bachelor boaters. That is, she supplies boatmen with women for their boats."

Bella laughed and looked at Roger.

"Do you suppose she'll send you a bill?"

"You little devil! You're the most surprising girl for a minister's daughter. I don't believe you'd mind if it was in the way of business."

Bella looked at him. In the light his close black curls were sculptured, his ear clear-cut as marble.

"I don't believe I should," she said honestly.

He leaned forward to arrange their blankets and realized that he held her hands.

They laughed again.

He let go her hands and spread the blankets so that they sat with their faces following the towrope, with the lantern light full on them.

She said, "It's private from the boat all right, but all the world could see us."

"The world's asleep, darling."

"Suppose the driver boy looked back?"

"Suppose he did?"

"Do you think he'd be upset if you kissed me, Roger?"

"Any man would be upset. That's why I married you."

"We could hold hands, though," Bella said demurely.

VII

*T*HE CANAL came towards them, evenly and quietly. They heard the wash against the bow and the whisper of the waterside weeds, arrowhead and dancegrass. They saw a rat swim out from the opposite shore and his eyes pick out the lantern light like two hot flecks of mica, and then he wheeled smoothly and paddled water till they passed. Once in a while they heard a boat horn, which the distance made sad; but at each succeeding blast it became louder and more dissonant, until at last they saw the light floating towards them, so slow, so easy, and so silent. And then they heard the panting of the team and saw them for a long instant in the lantern light: their hung heads and their lathered forelegs; their laboring sides; their bellies round and hard with strain; and their haunches riveted in thrust. Then the wash of the bows; and the boat's lantern light was married to the packet light; and their hands met under the blanket.

Sometimes the steersman of the passing boat noticed them. Then he said nothing; or he raised his arm, or made a buzzing noise in his horn like a bee buzzing in the trumpet of a lily; or he called good-night, or yodeled. But sometimes he never noticed them, and as the darkness redefined their lantern they kissed each other to reward his blindness. Sometimes their own steersman hailed the freight boat, and the two men bandied words a moment and left off, breaking a phrase.

Once they heard a bugle and saw the faster light of another packet. The driver boys cut at each other's teams, and their whips writhed into an embrace and fell apart. The boat came by with the ladies' windows darkened like their own, but one light burned in the saloon, and they saw two men throwing dice.

They watched the broad gleam from the doors of a change-stable beside the towpath, and saw the new team waiting and a boy ready-mounted, and a man standing behind them to catch the hook from the old team and fasten on the new. There was a smell of bedded horses as they passed the barn. The new team was linked to them in darkness as they moved, so that the boat never lost way.

They came into a lock, their bugle winging its notes far forward. The lock keeper had the level ready for them. He stood by the walking beam in his nightshirt, a lantern in his hand, a hat on his head, and his beard white as Noah's. The packet slid into the yawning gateway, which closed behind them, and the team rested while the water, like a hand, raised them up between the great gray blocks of stone until they saw the canal again faintly stretching from the opened gates and went away along it with the sound of the waste water on the tumbling bay.

They seemed to drift upon the water with a motion as unearthly as the wheel of the stars that traveled on the water with them. Bella felt herself grow sleepy without tiredness; she felt her husband's warmth steal into her, and her own warmth steal into his; and she thought, "I am his wife now," and she wished that she might be a good one to him, and it occurred to her that she was in love with him, and she wondered whether he was in love with her and whether he would love the things she loved.

She went with him on tiptoe into the saloon. There was a sound of snoring from Mr. Jason's bed. There was only a faint ring of yellow in the lamp chimney. But she saw the shoes of the men, and Mr. L. D. Jones's unconsumed segar, and she smelled men sleeping, and she was afraid for a minute; so, under cover of her cape, when they came to the ladies' door, she put both arms round Roger to make sure of him again.

But she felt ill at ease entering the ladies' cabin. Viney rolled the whites of her eyes and got up from her bed on the floor, breathing gently, and helped her to undress. The black hands made a mystery of the act.

The women looked gross in their blankets; Mrs. Neilson was noisy in her sleep, and Mrs. Cashdollar's red hair made a stain on the pillow.

"Good night, Viney," Bella whispered.

"Good night, Mis' Willcox."

The black hands, smoothing the blankets over her, were comforting. Bella turned her face to the wall and wept, being homesick.

VIII

WHEN Bella opened her eyes she thought that she had waked in Bedlam. The white wall beside her pillow was washed in sunlight, the air was warm and close. The cabin, except for herself, was empty.

But beyond the open windows was an uproar of strange noises—men bellowing oaths and a tremendous roaring of water and the stamp of mules and horses, and through it all came a persistent whir and clacking that she could not identify.

As she lay there, dazed with sleep, and still trying to sort the noises, the door opened and Viney slipped into the cabin.

"Good mornin', Mis' Willcox."

"Good morning, Viney. What on earth is all the noise about?"

"Oh, that!" Viney cocked her head backward on her thin neck and laughed. "We're in Little Falls and the captain's out on the towpath clearin' passage for us to the locks."

As she spoke the *Western Lion* jerked ahead. Bella gave a startled squeak as the side bumped

43

into another boat just opposite her head. Viney sprang to the window.

"We done bumped the crumbiest dirty old box you ever saw," she said delightedly. "Oh Lawd, Mis' Willcox, do come here. The captain's gettin' his mad up."

An explosion of profanity smothered all the shouting. Bella slid out of bed in her nightdress and took her place behind Viney at the window. The black girl crouched down to let her see and manipulated the curtains skillfully to screen her.

"Lawsy! Ain't he rarin'!"

"Where, Viney?"

"On the towpath, mis'. Just bend yo' head and look back."

Bella looked out on a scene of hopeless confusion. The towpath had given way to a stone parapet on which towing teams were crowded so close they seemed in danger of bumping each other over into the river that, by the roaring of the water, she could tell ran just below. Right and left, boats were lined up against the stonework, waiting their turn at the series of locks. To the left the red sides of a mill building rose close to the canal, and from its almost windowless interior issued the whirring and clacking of weaving machinery.

The packet boat was drifting slowly, losing way. The packet team stood nearly opposite Bella's window, with the towrope lying loose

44

over the back of a freight boat. The driver boy, white-faced and sleepy from his early morning ride, sat sidewise on his horse and looked back. And, looking back herself, Bella saw canallers, men and women together, crowding towards two men on the towpath. One of them was the captain, one hand holding down his beard to give his remarks free passage. The other was a round-shouldered, bearlike man, who pointed towards his almost paintless boat and clamored with monotonous hoarse anger for everyone to examine the damage.

The captain's face was flaming. Bella could not hear everything he shouted, but she could see his rage. Suddenly the crowd formed a ring about the two. Their faces looked eager. Some laughed. Some shouted for a fight.

But the freight boatman did not want a fight. He wanted damages. He repeated that. He pointed again at his boat.

"Just look there," he said. "Just look! Damn all packet boats and their damned lousy captains."

Behind him a woman screeched and threw her weight against his shoulders. The man lurched, tripped, and abruptly caught his balance. Bella gasped. The captain had brought him up on his feet with a solid smash to the mouth. The man stopped and spat. His spit was bloody.

A little boy who had shinnied up the bow standard of the boat next in line yelled at the top of his shrill voice: "Hey! Look at Georgie!" Another little boy, who was obviously Georgie, scampered along the embankment and thrust his head between the legs of a bystander. He was wearing an undershirt and nothing else, and the sun had made his tight little buttocks red.

Bella started to laugh. But her laughter broke, for now the fight was joined. The bearish man grunted and closed in. He had tremendous forearms, and his shoulders were bunched under his red undershirt. The captain met him with hard quick blows.

Bella heard the captain's fists strike into the man's face. She heard it over the roar of the river, and the whir of the mill machinery, and the muttering of the clustered freight boatmen. She had never seen two men fight before. She had never seen a human being badly hurt. Now she watched the packet captain carve the man's face. Her insides did funny things to her, but she could not look away.

The two men maneuvered very slowly, the freight boatman standing almost in one place and the captain shifting in a small circle. As the freight boatman's body came round, Bella saw his cheeks puffed and swollen, one eye half closed, a smear of red under his nose, and a broad trickle of blood running from the broken lips down his chin.

When he faced Bella, she saw his mind groping unsteadily with an idea as plainly as if the captain had opened up the man's brain for her inspection.

"Look out!"

Viney started and looked up at her, and Bella realized that the high voice was her own.

The man leaped. His fingers were hooked for the captain's face; but the captain had jumped back, and as the man ended his rush the captain started a swing from way back that traveled up like a scythe stroke and broke the man's face wide open. He went down where Bella could not see him.

The captain stood over him, panting and wiping his hands on his trousers.

"There's your damages, you dumb hog."

Somebody laughed. Then everybody laughed and a couple of boatmen shook the captain's hand. The captain laughed too. He caught sight of the snarled towrope and roared at the driver boy. But now his voice was hearty and without anger, and all freighters lent a hand in getting the packet free. Viney, giggling, whipped shut the curtains.

Bella was shaking, not from horror of what she had watched, but from sheer excitement. Viney exclaimed delightedly as she poured water in the washroom, "Didn't the captain jes' natchally lay him out?"

"Hurry, Viney."

"Yes, Mis' Willcox. The water's ready for you. It's spring water."

The water was icy cold against Bella's cheeks. "What time is it, Viney?"

"Most half-pas' seven, Mis' Willcox." Viney had the giggles again. "They was starting breakfas' when we came in here. But I reckon Mistah Willcox been awaiting you."

IX

IN THE saloon the beds had been put up for the day; the long tables had been set, and at one end the uncleared dishes of the other passengers were still in place. Bella realized that she was very late.

Mrs. Neilson was sitting in the library with an open prayer book on her knees and a newspaper in her hands. There was no one else. When Bella said good morning to her, she replied as if nothing out of the way had taken place. She said it seemed to be really quite a tolerably pleasant day.

Bella agreed cordially. Did Mrs. Neilson know where everybody was? "No," said Mrs. Neilson. She really couldn't say. They had gone on deck some time ago and that lazy steward had disappeared. The service on this boat was terrible.

It was quite obvious that Mrs. Neilson knew exactly what had taken place. Bella thought it more than likely she had been peering through the bull's-eye window.

She said, "I think I'll run on deck and see where my husband is."

"I shouldn't do that," said Mrs. Neilson, turning for support to Mr. Neilson, who just then came down.

"Good morning, Mrs. Willcox," he said. "No, I most certainly should advise against your going on deck. There's been—ah—a rather unpleasant contretemps."

"I'd say it was a damn good fight, myself." Mrs. Cashdollar blundered down behind the minister and patted her hair with satisfaction. "Oh, hello, dearie. Too bad you missed it. A boatman tried to block us from the lock. The captain had to beat him up."

"I saw it through the window," Bella said before she thought. She heard Mrs. Neilson's instant sibilant disapproval.

But Mrs. Cashdollar said heartily, "Did you, dearie? I need whiskey. Excitement's bad for me this early. Steward! Where in Halifax is that steward?" He appeared tardily. "Leave those dirty dishes, young man, and fetch me a whiskey. A small one. Don't put water in it."

She took the glass into the library and sat down opposite Mrs. Neilson, tilted her head, and let the whiskey slide.

"A drop in the bucket," she remarked. "Well, well. So you were watching from the cabin window, dearie? Did you see that big bezabor kiss the captain's hand?" she said to Bella. "Oh, here's your young man. He's been waiting breakfast

52

for you. You'd better sit down quick." She gave Roger a full smile.

Roger stood stiffly at the foot of the steps, listening to Mrs. Cashdollar's remarks and looking at Bella. Bella wanted to giggle. "I didn't know he could look down his nose like that," she thought, and went up to him. It wouldn't do to kiss him, but she would like to. Instead, she slipped her hand in his arm and said, "It was nice of you to wait for me."

They sat down at the far end of the table. Opening her peach, Bella wondered whether he would always look down his nose before breakfast and asked him how he had slept.

"Not much," he said.

"I slept beautifully," she said. "I didn't expect to, though."

Roger said he was glad. His voice was perfunctory. He was peeling his peach slowly and carefully with his strong hands. "He's so neat," she thought. "Look at the mess I've made of mine." She felt how improper she was and wanted to giggle again. She couldn't help thinking what fun it would be to ask him if he didn't think the captain's fight had been glorious.

But he said suddenly, "Too bad about that fuss. The captain had to do it, but I was afraid it might upset you."

She said, which was true, "I was just waking up." He could set that against Mrs. Cashdollar's remarks if he wanted to. But she noticed with relief that by the time he had eaten one egg he was no longer looking down his nose.

"I must see that breakfast is on time in our house," she said to herself. "*Always!*"

X

*T*HE Little Falls packet dock was situated above the locks and close to the entrance of the feeder aqueduct. The *Western Lion* tied up there for five minutes to take on two passengers, a Mr. and Mrs. Ransom. They had descended from a smart carriage and pair and booked passage for Syracuse. Mrs. Ransom brought an atmosphere of refinement into the saloon, and Bella instinctively classed them both as gentlefolk with Roger, Mr. Atterbury, and herself.

Mrs. Ransom said good morning all round with a gracious lack of discrimination that Mrs. Neilson seemed to find nettling. She immediately asked whether Mrs. Ransom had enjoyed breakfast yet, and, finding she had, asked if she could help her to select a bed. Mrs. Ransom thanked her kindly, but replied that, as she felt rather fatigued, she would prefer to sit in the shady corner of the library to wait until Mr. Ransom came down. She retired behind the *North American Review*. Mrs. Neilson forced a smile. But she made a remark to Mrs. Cashdollar which seemed to amuse that lady very much. It was obvious that Mrs. Neilson had tried to put herself and Mrs. Ransom in a separate class, that she had failed in her first attempt, and that she didn't like it at all.

On deck, Bella found the air warm but bracing. A west wind was sweeping down the valley carrying clouds that drew their shadows over the steep flanks of the hills. Sheep drifted on the upland pastures. Men were reaping in the river flats, while behind them the bent forms of women bound the sheaves and set the shocks in files. There seemed to be movement over all the earth, as though the wind had wakened every living thing.

As Bella walked up and down between Roger and Mr. Atterbury, she was made conscious again of the delightful ease of packet traveling. There was no jolting, no dust, no smell of horses. The motion of the boat was unwavering; it went so steadily that the towing team and the long curving towrope lost their visible relation to the journey. The narrow bright blue ribbon of the canal was like a scroll, unwinding west along the valley, the boat a picture painted on it, herself and Roger portraits of a bridal pair.

The ribbons down the sides of Bella's dove-gray traveling dress fluttered gayly, and the silk covering of her parasol snapped like a pigeon's wings. Though she sauntered with demureness back and forth along the fifty feet of deck, she longed to jump ashore, to lift her skirts and run a race with the packet, with Roger, with the wind.

A hawk, his wings two swords against the sky, roused envy in her. He needed no boat to take his way across the earth. As she lifted her eyes to follow the keen flight, the wind blew her bonnet ribbons over her lips, and under cover of untangling them she kissed her fingers.

Mr. Atterbury's alert eyes caught the gesture. She saw him smile, and she glanced hastily at Roger. But Roger was watching the country, not the sky. And she cried to him, "Look, Roger. The hawk."

She did not need to point; he had good eyes. He found the bird at once.

"He'd make a long shot."

Bella said, "I wouldn't want him shot. I wish I were him."

"Why?"

"To fly, Roger."

"Where would you fly to?"

"Away. Anywhere. It wouldn't matter. Only fly."

She looked so eager.

"Away from me?" he asked, grinning.

"Yes. If you loved me you'd grow your own wings."

She said it lightly, but she was annoyed. She did not want to be made fun of by Roger. Mr. Atterbury understood what she meant. She could

tell that by the way he looked at her. He too was smiling, but his smile was to himself.

Roger said, "Look at your hawk now. Do you still like him?"

He pointed. The hawk had bounded a hundred feet, breast to the wind, his wings like tempered steel. He was keeping an exact spot in the blue. His wings fluttered, lightly touching the wind. Then they slid back and his body, a gray arrow, stooped to the river's edge.

"Watch," said Roger.

A thin metallic scream issued from the grass. A moment later they saw the hawk rise again, thrusting steadily with his wings, his legs straight down, and a brown shape swinging in his talons.

But Bella did not care about a dead water rat. Her eyes followed the magnificent towering climb, up and up, until the hawk had gained the level of the highest hill. Against the sky she could not see the bird move, but his shape dwindled until it was a speck.

Bella's glance swung challengingly round on Roger. She had forgotten Mr. Atterbury. She had forgotten everyone but herself and Roger, earth-bound, moving four miles an hour, on their pitiful twelve-by-fifty feet of packet deck. He was still grinning at her.

"I thought you hated rats," he said.

The steersman, leaning idly against the rudder stick, stared between them with a blank face.

"Let's stop talking about him," Bella said.

XI

*B*RIDGE."

"Low bridge."

Bella turned on her heel, and the wind met her lips as she faced westward.

The team, a gray led by a black, were trotting into the arched shadow. The white timbers framed a circle of blue—blue sky and blue water in which they were reflected. The horses passed out of sight beyond the abutment timbers, then returned to the frame at the end of the towrope, treading above their own reflections, with the driver boy's jacket a scarlet bud against a line of willows.

Bella was by herself. She had been cross with Roger. She wouldn't talk to him. He wouldn't even get angry, and after ten minutes of it he had left her, going below.

She glanced quickly fore and aft. She did not want to go down on the steersman's deck. Mr. Jason was standing there, confabulating with the steersman in an offhand voice.

Bella knew that she was involved in their conversation. Both of them had been amused when

Roger stalked down into the saloon. The steersman looked red in the face when she met his eye; but Mr. Jason stared right back. Then his eyes embarked on a tour of inspection of her person, speculative, probing, vulgar.

But the bridge timbers were looming over the boat's course.

"I don't care what they think," she said to herself.

She ran forward swiftly and looked over. At the sound of her footfall Mr. Atterbury's hat appeared. He touched the brim with his fingers. Seeing that she was going to jump, he pointed to what she had missed in the darkness last night, a small ladder leading from the corner of the saloon deck to the catwalk. She had just time to step over, step down, meeting his fingers with hers, and step round the corner of the ladies' cabin to the deck. The bridge shadows swept over her with the cool echoing sound of water lapping against wood. Mr. Jason's sudden laugh sounded obscene. She flushed, bit her lip, and said to Mr. Atterbury, "I don't like that man."

"Nor I," said Mr. Atterbury. "But when you travel in this country you must make up your mind to put up with his genus. They are regrettably plentiful."

"I suppose so," Bella said. "But I don't like him at all. What do you suppose he does?"

"Land speculator, probably."

"Oh?"

Mr. Atterbury elaborated: "He probably runs or works for a company that buys up tracts of poor land and advertises them in the East—or, better yet, in Europe—selling them sight unseen to credulous poor souls."

The steward had set out some chairs on the deck. Bella and Mr. Atterbury seated themselves.

"I hope you don't object to my segar, Mrs. Willcox."

"No, not at all. I love the smell of fine tobacco."

She leaned a little forward, letting her wrists lie on her knees. Pulling smoothly at his segar, Mr. Atterbury appreciatively studied her. She had a pliant, graceful back, and slim, youthful arms. The dove-gray dress, fitting snugly, was particularly becoming. Her leghorn bonnet, with its demure Quakerish crown and the visor decked with most unquakerish ribbons, was drawn low on her brown hair. Even in the shadow of it her small face was bright with her resentment of Mr. Jason. "Spunky," Mr. Atterbury said to himself, seeing the little pucker of her brow. She looked delicious when she frowned. Her lower lip became sullen; she did not seem quite so indecently young and innocent to be a married woman. He sighed. Parents, he thought, had no business letting their daughters marry out of sheltered households at Bella Willcox's age; but he thought indulgently of them, also knowing that it was this youthful innocence that made her so delightful a study for an old man. It wasn't the world she was making acquaintance of—that would come later; it was herself.

He sighed again. She was trying to make easy conversation. She wanted to appear mature. Well, it was only fair to let her gain confidence. She would need it, poor pretty child, he thought. It seemed a pity that all her awakening fire should be wasted on a young man who quite obviously could not appreciate what was taking place.

"Yes, Mrs. Willcox," he said, rousing his tongue. "I suppose I have traveled about a good deal. I probably bored you and your husband half to death last evening. But old men become garrulous, you know."

"Oh, no indeed, Mr. Atterbury. I never listened to anyone so interesting."

"You flatter me, my dear. I get fits of running on sometimes, and hardly know what I'm saying."

She glanced at his shrewd eyes.

"I don't believe that. But I wish you'd run on some more, anyway. You said something last night about being held up on the highroad by the queerest man you'd ever met. I was dying to know who he was."

"Were you?" He smiled. "I'll wager you forgot all about him ten seconds after you left the saloon."

She blushed, and then annoyance at acting so youthfully made her blush deeper.

"If I did," she said, smiling back at him, "I didn't forget it for keeps, did I?"

Her honesty delighted him.

"Just for that, I'll tell you. The highwayman was a Mr. St. Clair of the very finest Virginia stock. The highroad would have served much better as a bridle path than as a stage road. I was on my way from Nashville in Tennessee to Memphis. I was a good deal younger then, and no doubt I was singing a song, or filling my head with thoughts of the company I had parted with in Nashville, which was very pleasant, though I've never had opportunity to renew it. I dare say I wasn't paying much attention to the road."

Mr. Atterbury's eyes rested kindly on Bella's face; but he did not seem to see her, and she thought, "Maybe I'm making him remember some other woman."

"I had—it sounds preposterous—eleven hundred dollars in a belt around my waist, the result of a lucky investment in Nashville. But I was a chuckle-headed boy in those days and thought I could take care of myself anywhere. I got a jolt when my horse reared; and when I got him in hand I found I was looking right into the business end of a horse pistol.

"He was very handsomely dressed," continued Mr. Atterbury, drawing smoothly on his segar, "for a man in those lonely districts. He was clean-shaven, and I saw at a glance that he was a gentleman. But I was badly rattled, and I lifted my hands at once."

Mr. Atterbury laughed so infectiously at the recollection that Bella could not help joining in.

"Did he rob you?" she asked.

"Technically. But not of my money. He robbed me of an evening's conversation. He never gave me a chance to say a word until he had ridden me ahead of him for a mile or so down a narrow by-path. Then he said, 'Now, sir, we're safe from interference and we'd better come to an understanding.' I looked back over my shoulder and thought it was all up. He still had the pistol aimed square at me, and he had a devilishly steady hand. He said, 'May I enquire your name, sir?' I told him, and he bowed over his horse's withers. 'Reginald St. Clair, sir, of Magnolia Grove, Hardeman County.' So I bowed. And he said, 'I am obliged to disconvenience you, Mr. Atterbury. I'm a lonely man, and I am forced to collect company as I am able. If you'll resume your ride, we've only a mile to go, sir.'"

Mr. Atterbury chuckled to himself.

"He was a fine fellow. And he had elegant manners."

"He didn't touch your money, then?" Bella asked.

"Good heavens no, my dear. He gave me as good a dinner as I've ever sat down to. He had a beautiful house and a fine plantation and a plenty of slaves. But he felt that the vicinity was too

lonely to bring a lady to, so he lived by himself."
Mr. Atterbury sighed reminiscently. "Luckily
he had no such compunctions about his cook. I
enjoyed every mouthful. I slept in a four-post
feather bed on lavendered sheets. In the morning
he took me back to the highroad and sent me
on to the next village with two of his Negroes,
armed, for an escort."

"I wish I were a man," Bella said, drawing a
deep breath.

"You'd make a pretty gentleman, my dear. But
if you were, in bare justice to your new sex, you'd
have to wish yourself a woman again."

Bella lifted her hands and rested her chin on
them.

"If I *were* a man I wonder if I would like
women."

"Pretty women," said Mr. Atterbury.

"Blonde ones, I think. And I'd treat them
heartlessly."

Mr. Atterbury pulled on his segar.

"Well, for Mr. Willcox's sake I hope you'll
never have the opportunity to find out."

Bella laughed.

"Oh, Roger. He wants a girl to be small and
fluffy, with lots of lacy clothes, I think."

"It's a practically universal taste among men.
Good ones, too."

"He was very stuffy this morning," Bella said.
"He didn't seem to like anything I said."

"You mustn't let it trouble you, my dear. You know it takes a good many years for a young man to discover he hasn't married a valentine in a lace envelope." Mr. Atterbury smiled. "He's a nice young man, but I'm sure you'll shock him a good many times."

"*I* shock *him?*"

"Yes, my dear. It's much easier to shock men than women, I've found. And you see you're a very genuine person and not at all a copybook young lady."

Bella said ruefully, "I know it. My sister is different, though. She takes such pains with things. But then, it's worth while for her. She's lovely-looking."

She felt a pleased little tremor take hold of her as she encountered Mr. Atterbury's eyes. They were remarkably young for a man with white hair, she thought.

"You know, Mr. Atterbury, I watched that fight this morning. And I wasn't shocked. I loved it!"

He nodded. "I'm not surprised. But it doesn't mean that your heart is any the less gentle, my dear."

"Mine wasn't gentle a bit."

He seemed amused at her vehemence.

"And yet here you are getting yourself all upset over that big husband of yours just because he teased you."

"I'm not upset. I don't see why he should get stuffy just because I feel so wonderfully."

"My dear child, you've just been set free in the world." Mr. Atterbury's kindly smile robbed his words of all offense. "But your husband has just been caught. And you see, he has no resource."

"Resource?" Bella turned to him. Then she flushed. "I see what you mean. But that's silly."

"No, it isn't. You haven't any idea. You've showed that already." He blew a stream of segar smoke. "I hate to think how I'd behave in his shoes."

He tactfully examined the ash of his segar.

"Oh," Bella said in a muffled voice. She stared forward along the canal. After a while she asked, "What can I do?"

"If you want advice, I'd suggest distraction for Mr. Willcox. Maybe you can plead a headache or some indisposition this evening, and don't let him take you on deck."

"The cabin's so stuffy with Mrs. Neilson in it."

Mr. Atterbury laughed.

"I'll bet it is. But lots of things are stuffy."

"Well, I'll do it. Though I don't see how it can help much."

"I'll try to amuse him with other things."

"Could you?"

Mr. Atterbury accepted the naïve question with forbearance.

"Backgammon—or maybe I could arrange a small game of cards."

Bella was interested at once.

"Oh, Roger would like that. He loves cards. I believe he plays very well."

"Does he? That's fine."

"It's very kind of you."

"Pshaw. I'd enjoy it myself."

"But it is."

"Not at all, my dear."

Mr. Atterbury leaned forward and laid his hand over hers.

"Don't worry," he said.

She thought nobody could have been kinder, and at lunch she was particularly nice to Roger.

XII

*M*RS. Cashdollar had brought up her bags. She stood by the steersman with Bella, watching the town draw nearer, while, level with her eyes, the feet of Roger and Mr. Atterbury walked briskly up and down the saloon deck.

"I always like to come up when I get to my own home town," Mrs. Cashdollar said. "It's pretty coming into it on a canalboat."

Utica lay ahead. Against the bright blue sky it did look inviting, with its tall buildings, some of them five stories high, its white church steeples, its glittering, gilded weather vanes.

"Don't it strike you pretty, Jake?"

Mrs. Cashdollar was familiar with the steersman. They had done business together once. But the steersman replied guardedly, "Utica is a nice enough town, Lucy; but it's got the most consarned crowded basin on the line."

The captain appeared on deck, roaring at the driver boy to tickle some style into the team, and the driver boy cursed and lashed with a show of zeal. The captain pulled out his watch. "Twenty minutes," he said calculatingly. "I ain't going to wait for passengers. I'm out for a record. If they don't show up they can wait or they can walk."

"A record?" Bella asked. "Why do you want to make one?"

"Stage lines have cut their rates," the captain explained. "We're still under them. We throw in food on the price of the ticket. But people want speed nowadays, ma'am. By God, the Red Bird Line's going to give it to them, too." He smiled patronizingly. "You don't realize it, ma'am, but you've been travel-  ing a dang sight better than four miles an hour."

The canal slanted away from the river to- wards the heart of Uti- ca. The packet passed a drag of four cribs of scantling chained to- gether. The last crib had a kind of ramshackle hut on it, and three nearly naked men with poles kept fending the drag from the banks. They looked wild and partly drunk, and they cheered raucously as the packet went by.

After the *Western Lion* passed the lumber, though it had the canal to itself for a short way, the captain jumped up on the saloon deck and began blowing his bugle: "Yankee Doodle," and the "Irish Washerwoman," and "Anacreon in Heaven." The notes soared away and the brightness of the music in the bright air pricked even the horses' ears.

"He's warning the weighlock," explained the steersman. "They'll have the level ready and the gates open and hold back the freights for us."

The *Western Lion* glided suddenly into the shadow of a house; the canal narrowed. A garden fence stood right upon the bank, and the thud of hoofs echoed against wood walls. The bugle notes seemed to shoot away with redoubled volume. A window opened and a maid looked forth and waved a duster. Two little black children screamed and chased the boat and did fancy steps for pennies.

Bella looked at the backs of the houses. Trees grew over the fences; she smelled blooming phlox above the stale smell of the canal water. Slanted avenues of sunlight succeeded shadows and put enchantment on the women's dresses, so that even the incredible display Mrs. Cashdollar wore was made attractive.

"You can get up on top now," the steersman said after they emerged from the shadow of another bridge. "It's free from here to the packet dock."

They mounted, Bella and Mrs. Cashdollar, the Ransoms and the Neilsons, joining Mr. Atterbury, the captain, and Roger. Mrs. Cashdollar touched Bella's elbow. Bella started. She had been traveling in enchantment for an instant, not realizing how short a time it was since she had seen the signs and smelled the smells of people living close together along city streets; it seemed ages ago.

She turned to find Mrs. Cashdollar studying her with unaccustomed diffidence.

"I just wanted to say, dearie, I hope you'll be happy. You've got a nice boy. Stick to him tight."

"Thank you," said Bella.

The woman's painted face looked sentimental.

Then she faced ahead.

"It's pretty, ain't it?"

They were in a belt of shadow, and already the noise of the basin hung dimly before them like a drone of swarming bees. The scent from a rose garden hung in the shadow, and the clear voice of a young woman calling a child.

Then the captain again blew on his bugle. They emerged into blistering sunlight. Bella saw boats lined up along the towpath, beyond them a square building, housing the canal like a tunnel, and a group of men all staring towards the *Western Lion.*

The driver boy yelled backward, "Mind your step, George."

"Slog ahead," roared the steersman.

The packet seemed to pick up speed. The rope, now passed over the standard in the bow, remained taut. The packet swung into the middle of the canal, slowly, tensely, until, when the bow straightened, they were aimed for the weighlock like thread for a needle's eye.

For a breathless instant Bella felt her heart constrict. Suppose they struck. But she knew they would not. The team plunged through with a deafening thunder of hoofs on the plank run. The packet slid in and out again, and the sunlight suddenly dazzled her. The steersman was nonchalantly leaning on the rudder stick. He arched a spit, then wiped his mouth, and with the gesture dropped his hand to the stick, bore on it, and the boat eased into the packet dock like a feat of magic. Handlers caught the ropes and snubbed them fast to the ties; the gang clattered down. And Mrs. Cashdollar was saying good-bye as if the whole display had been contrived expressly for her return to Utica.

XIII

*B*ELLA lay stiff on her back, her hands under her neck, her eyes closed, pretending to sleep. Mrs. Neilson, who had had more than the usual port at supper, had mercifully dropped off; but when Bella peered through her lashes she discovered Mrs. Ransom's eyes turned meditatively in her direction.

Bella did not feel like talking. She lay quiet, her nerves on stretch. She would have liked to get up, to move about the cabin, to lean out of a window. It was almost airless in the cabin—the circle of light in the lamp chimney burned blue, as if the flame found insufficient oxygen. The curtains hung limp, though every window was wide. Outside the blackness was unbroken. There were not even stars tonight.

They had passed no locks, for the packet was still on the Long Level, which extended from Frankfort to Syracuse. The *Western Lion* had drawn through Rome at sunset, and the captain had then said that Rome was halfway on the Level. Now they were in the black-snake section of the canal, winding through hemlock and bal-

sam swamps and long open bogs. Frogs made a
continual bellowing that traveled with the boat,
drowning all smaller sounds, until Bella felt the
blood beating in her head.

She tried to make herself sleep by thinking
of her family in Albany, but the scenes were
blurred, and through them the faces of Roger and
Mr. Atterbury kept emerging—one grinning
and mocking, the other keen, and both watching her while she followed the free flight of the
hawk.

After putting the washroom to rights, Viney
came into the cabin. She moved with the casual
stealth of a wild animal and made her bed upon

the floor without a sound. She curled up on the pallet, one thin arm outstretched across the boards, the other curved across her face, her mouth opening a little for a long silent exhalation.

The boat slid onward through the rumbling of the bullfrogs. There were no bridges any more to raise the driver's cry. There had been no lights for an hour, except one passing glow from another boat, more lonely in the darkness than the night itself.

Bella felt afraid.

She did not know why, but her mind turned suddenly towards her future. For the first time it occurred to her to wonder what living with Roger was going to be like: sharing her bed with him, feeling the beat of his heart, hearing him breathe, seeing him in the morning when he woke, having to dress and undress in his sight. A wave of nausea swept over her. She could smell the saloon again as it had been last night, heavy from the breathing of men and the deadness of Mr. L. D. Jones's segar. She shivered and felt sweat on her forehead.

"Don't be a fool," she said to herself. "I wanted him. I wanted him from the beginning." Roger was not like that. He was very clean. He never smelled of staleness. The skin on his wrists was very white. "I'm going to make him happy and be happy." She said it with her teeth clenched.

She was thinking of a time when, as a little girl, she had been on her uncle's farm outside the city, and she and Clorinda had stolen off to the barn mow to see one of the mares served. She had heard her uncle talking about it with one of the hands, and she and Clorinda had thought it would be enchanting to see a horse being served. They had climbed up the ladder and looked into the paddock through a crack in the hay door. They could see far out from there over the country, and they were hardly settled before they spied a little man leading a big black horse along the road. They had wondered what that horse was coming for and kept watching for the mare. They knew her very well, having often stolen carrots from the kitchen garden for her. But the little man kept leading the black horse along, and he turned with him into the paddock, and the horse had put up his crest and neighed, and it was then that the mare appeared. They brought the bay mare into the paddock.

Before that Bella had always thought of her as a fine, spirited animal, but now she seemed to have lost all courage. Clorinda had asked what was going to happen. Clorinda had been all eyes when the men put the mare into the paddock. But Bella had been sick. When she was through being sick, the mare was back in the stable, and the men were out by the gate, laughing a little. The stallion was going back down the road, by the way he had come, making play on the halter, so that the little man seemed light on his toes, like a dancer. It had been a bright sunny day with a sweeping wind. She remembered how the stallion's mane had blown forward as he walked.

Outside a boat horn blared, and Bella lay still. It was so near that almost immediately she heard the team on the towpath; and then the light came by. She wondered whether she had been asleep and missed the first note of the horn.

With the passage of the freight boat, silence crept into the cabin again. Then through the wall at her head she heard the dim sounds of the men's voices. They were playing a long game.

Mr. Atterbury had made his suggestion to Roger before supper, but Roger had consulted her privately before agreeing. She was glad he had. But she pleaded a headache and said she would prefer to go to bed early. She had not realized then how hot it would be in the ladies' cabin. She had counted on having it to herself for a while; but as soon as the other ladies had seen that Mr. Atterbury was getting up a game of cards they had followed her example, and now she was trapped.

The sound of cards irritated her with its persistence. She thought resentfully of Roger's pleasure at the idea. He had, of course, been solicitous about her headache, and he had been attentive all through supper. But he had not suggested that fresh air would be better for a head-ache.

He was fond of cards. Maybe it was only fair that he should have a game—he had been sub-merged for so long by all her relations and the frilleries of getting married in a respectable fam-ily. But it did not seem fair either that she should have to be cooped up in this stuffy box of a cabin with two women, one of whom snored.

Mrs. Neilson was not snoring, but Bella thought it was only a matter of time before she would start.

"I just can't stand it if she does," she thought.

She lay quite still, and little by little the dark-ness came in upon her through the airless win-dows with the clamor of the frogs. After a while she wondered whether Mrs. Ransom had gone to sleep. She opened her eyes and carefully looked through her lashes.

Mrs. Ransom was still sitting up in bed with her face turned to the open window. Her hair was loose on her shoulders. It had streaks of gray growing back from the temples, but they hardly showed across the cabin. Her absorption made her face look young.

Bella was surprised to see what a pretty night-gown Mrs. Ransom was wearing. Not at all what she would have expected—nothing like her moth-er's staid garments that laced tight round the neck and had half sleeves in summer, full in winter. Mrs. Ransom's was low-cut and edged with lace. It was cut far lower than Bella's own. Through it her breast shone under the lamp with a clean soft line.

"Why," thought Bella, "she looks beautiful."

She let her eyelids droop. Mrs. Ransom had been smiling, and a sixth sense made her aware that Mrs. Ransom had been looking at her just before she opened her eyes. . . .

XIV

*T*HROUGH the wall she heard one of the men laugh. She was not positive, but it had sounded like Roger's voice. It had sounded forced, though. She held her breath. The men were silent now. Then she heard the chink of silver on the table. She realized that they were playing for money.

She had never thought of their playing for money. That was not right. She had never believed that playing cards was as sinful as her family maintained, so she had not felt shocked when Mr. Atterbury made his suggestion. But this was gambling.

To her surprise she found that she was sitting straight up in bed and that Mrs. Ransom was looking across at her.

"Can't you sleep, either?" Mrs. Ransom asked after a quick glance at Mrs. Neilson.

Bella could not answer.

Mrs. Ransom regarded her steadily for a minute, then slipped from bed and tiptoed across the cabin.

"What's the matter, my dear? Do you feel ill?"

Bella shook her head.

"Something's the matter."

"I'm afraid," Bella said. "I can't bear it any more in here."

"It's terribly close. But wait a minute."

Mrs. Ransom went back to her bed and returned with a bottle of smelling salts.

"Sniff this."

Bella obeyed. But the ammonia only served to clear her head. Again she heard the terrifying chink of money.

"Do you hear?"

Mrs. Ransom nodded. "They're still playing."

"But they're playing for money!"

"Is that what's worrying you?"

Mrs. Ransom smiled, and Bella felt better. Mrs. Ransom wasn't upset.

"Why shouldn't they play for money?" Mrs. Ransom asked. "It's theirs."

Bella tried to laugh.

"I guess I've been silly."

"Not quite."

Mrs. Ransom implied nothing. Her face was thoughtful. Then she looked at Mrs. Neilson's huddled form.

"I've been dying to get out of here myself. I wonder if we couldn't."

Bella said, "We couldn't go through the saloon."

"No, but we might get out the window."

Her eyes had a mischievous light. She seemed like another girl to Bella.

"Yes, let's," Bella whispered, slipping from her bed.

"Are you going to dress?" Mrs. Ransom asked.

"Oughtn't I?"

"I couldn't bear the feeling of clothes tonight."

"But we ought to put on something."

"You young people are always so proper," said Mrs. Ransom. "Well, maybe we ought to wear our cloaks. We'll have to protect ourselves from the mosquitoes, I suppose."

She got her cloak and slipped it over her nightgown. Then she stole back to Bella. They looked down at Viney. The black girl was stretched on her pallet, one arm still outflung above her kinky hair.

"Viney."

She opened her eyes instantly and sat up.

"See if you can help us through the window and pass us some blankets and two pillows without waking Mrs. Neilson."

Viney grinned. She led the way to a side window and poked out her head.

"Ain' nobody on deck, Mis' Ransom."

Mrs. Ransom pulled up her nightdress and stuck a slippered foot over the sill. In a moment, with surprising suppleness, she was through. Bella followed. Viney handed out the pillows and blankets and looked at them enviously.

"Don't you want to come, Viney?"

"Yes, mis'. I sho'ly does. But she'd wake if I wasn't here and call the captain."

Bella felt Mrs. Ransom take her hand.

"The steersman won't see us if we keep our heads down."

Mrs. Ransom went along the catwalk on hands and knees. When Bella joined her on the bow deck, she was laughing softly.

"The driver hasn't looked back. Once we're wrapped up, we'll look perfectly respectable."

They made themselves a place between the windows with their backs to the cabin wall, as Bella and Roger had on the preceding night.

It was much cooler outside, and the sound of the frogs, strangely, did not seem so deafening. The woods looked near and black, but far back in them fireflies were carrying lanterns. The sparks moved here and there, tracing patterns, and giving the night depth.

"I think we'll have a thunderstorm," said Mrs. Ransom.

Bella nodded.

XV

*U*NDER the folds of her cloak, Mrs. Ransom hugged her knees. Her throat made a clear, youthful line to the tilted chin. Bella thought she had never seen anyone more beautiful—not even Clorinda. Clorinda always gave one a sense of coolness; but Mrs. Ransom had warmth and sympathy under her unruffled poise. She shifted herself to lean lightly against Bella's shoulder, and as she did so a faint sweet perfume came from her.

"That's a lovely scent," Bella said. "Do you mind telling me what it is?"

Mrs. Ransom lowered her face. The mischievous light had left her eyes; they seemed somnolent and much darker.

"Not at all. It's Palm of Roses. My husband is very partial to it."

Bella made a mental note of the name. Her parents had always discouraged the use of perfume.

"I'm glad you like it," Mrs. Ransom went on. "If you'd like to try it, I'll give you a bottle. I've some extra."

"Thank you, I'd love it," Bella said. "I've never been allowed to have any."

Mrs. Ransom smiled.

"You're just married, aren't you, my dear?"

Bella nodded.

"George and I thought so. It made us both feel as if we were on a second honeymoon ourselves. We've decided to go off somewhere after his business is finished in Syracuse."

Bella asked, "Have you been married long?"

"It doesn't seem so tonight. But as a matter of fact we were married more than twenty years ago. I was hardly seventeen."

"Were you?" Bella looked at her.

Mrs. Ransom was silent.

Bella asked, "Were you ever frightened then? I don't mean really scared—" Her voice broke off.

"When? Oh, then? No, not really, I suppose. I was terribly excited. We went to Trenton Falls in a stage."

"We're going to Niagara Falls."

"That's nice. Aren't you a lucky girl! We spent two weeks at Trenton Falls. I had the most marvelous time. Are you frightened, my dear?"

"I don't know."

"You mustn't be. Your husband seems a fine young man."

"He is," Bella said stoutly. "I'm terribly in love with him. I'm not frightened that way. It's myself."

"I understand. Only I wasn't frightened. I didn't care. It seems to me I forgot I was a lady when the wedding ring went over my finger. And I've never quite managed to feel like one since. Do you know, I've always thought of my girlhood as being like a cut flower in a vase, kept in a shady corner of the best parlor and watered every day to keep me fresh."

"Oh not—not that!" Bella's voice was troubled. "It's only that I'm not sure of myself, and Roger."

"You won't be sure of anything till you've had a baby."

"Have you had any?"

"Five."

"I want a big family, too." Bella was very serious. "And I'm not going to treat the girls like dolls, either."

"You don't have to, if you live in the country the way we do. Hideous, noisy little guttersnipes, my relatives thought mine were. Perhaps they were right. But they're turning out quite nice now that they're growing up."

"We're going to live in Pittsburgh."

"Are you?"

"Yes, Roger works there in his father's business. He hasn't much of a salary, but his father is giving us our house, and Roger's managed to save enough for our honeymoon."

"You've never been west?"

"No."

"It's an adventure."

"Yes. I'm terribly excited. I hope his family will like me."

"Of course they'll like you."

Far down the line they heard a boat horn. Then they saw the light on their left through the trees. The boat came to them round a wide bend. The driver looked at them silently from beside his team. In the cabin they heard a man's voice and a woman crying.

"When I said I was afraid," Bella said in a small voice, "I meant I didn't know whether I was really in love with Roger."

"Don't worry," said Mrs. Ransom.

"But what could I do if I wasn't?"

"Don't worry."

"Roger seems different since yesterday."

Mrs. Ransom said gently, "He doesn't seem so wonderful or wise?"

Bella nodded.

"My dear, doesn't that make him all the more worth loving?"

Bella felt tears close under her lids. She could not speak.

"He's almost as young and maybe he's just as worried as you are." Mrs. Ransom's hand moved over hers.

"Oh, but it's not really the same," said Bella.

"Why not? He's been brought up with much

the same ideas you have. And now he finds he's got a live woman on his hands. And as long as he's on this boat he doesn't know."

The boat went on in stillness. In the south, lightning forked through a cloud. There was no thunder.

Behind them voices broke out in the saloon. They heard a short rueful laugh.

"It sounds as if the game were breaking up."

"I'm glad," said Bella.

"Still worried about your husband's playing for money?"

"A little."

"My dear, all men gamble. If they didn't you wouldn't be here now."

Bella laughed.

"We're worse than they, aren't we?"

"A hundred times. And willing to cheat any amount to win."

"You've won, haven't you?"

"It took me a good many years before I was sure of it."

Bella did not quite understand Mrs. Ransom's tone, but she felt indescribably comforted. She lay back and closed her eyes. She heard a dim mutter of thunder, but it was far away.

XVI

*I*T WAS much later when she woke. She found Mrs. Ransom's arm about her and her hand lightly upon her mouth.

"Hush."

Mrs. Ransom whispered close to her ear.

"Don't move."

Bella opened her eyes. They had just passed a relay stable, and the boat was moving slowly once more into darkness. Somewhere behind her she heard water running.

"We've passed Limestone Creek."

Bella nodded. She did not know where that was, but she understood the need of quiet, for she heard footsteps on the saloon deck behind her head. Two men were talking. One of the voices belonged to Mr. Jason.

"How much did we make?"

"About a hundred and fifty dollars, adding yours to mine."

"It was easy as dealing faro to a pair of frogs."

Mr. Atterbury laughed.

"L. D. Jones backed out, though," he added more soberly.

"I guess he got suspicious."

"He can't prove anything, and he's scared."

"What'll we do?"

"If it wasn't for Jones, I'd say hang on till Buffalo."

"Jones makes it bad. I guess we'd better jump boat."

"I'm afraid so."

Bella felt herself frozen. She heard, but even yet she hardly understood.

Mr. Jason made a snickering sound.

"Don't want to, hey? I saw you confab with that Willcox girl. She don't like me much, though."

"All right, Jason."

"Oh, all right. But she's a neat piece of goods. Why don't you try to take her along?"

"Shut up."

"All right, all right. You've got his money anyway. Though I don't see why you passed him the last hand that way."

"We decided to stop at a hundred and fifty. That's out of Ransom's pocket. You don't lose anything."

"It's a damn waste." Jason's voice was sour. But Bella heard no more. The men were moving back softly towards the steersman. There was a moment's colloquy. Then the boat swung gently in towards the bank. It barely touched, letting the grass scrape along the side.

Mrs. Ransom's hand squeezed Bella's tight as

they swung back into midstream. They had both heard the men light on the towpath.

"Well, my dear," said Mrs. Ransom.

Bella looked up at her.

"A hundred and fifty dollars!"

"That's good-bye to our trip," Mrs. Ransom said.

Bella wanted to cry. Poor Roger. Suddenly she remembered Jason's grumbling.

"Roger will have to pay that last hand back to Mr. Ransom."

"Why should he?"

"He didn't win it honestly."

"Nonsense, my dear. We've had our honeymoon. If your husband hadn't won it, you'd have to go straight on to Pittsburgh."

"That doesn't matter."

"But he was perfectly honest. Besides, I'm used to it now. My husband has one weakness. That's why we've made our home in the country. We both know it and avoid it as well as we can. It was only business that brought us on this trip. You mustn't be upset," said Mrs. Ransom. "George will be very nice to me after his 'bad luck.' "

"No," said Bella, "I can't allow it."

"Yes, you can. I'll tell you what. I want to make you a present of your honeymoon. There! In memory of my own."

Bella stared hard at her. Mrs. Ransom was looking out again at the darkness above the bow lantern. She told the truth—Bella felt sure of that. She felt very humble.

"Thank you."

Mrs. Ransom leaned towards Bella, her eyes tender, and kissed her.

"Don't worry, my dear."

Bella said she wouldn't.

The lightning forked brighter.

"We'd better go in."

Suddenly a puff of wind snatched a ripple from the canal. They stole into the window and handed Viney the blankets to fold. Lightning played beyond the window slats. Thunder rolled across the woods.

When Bella finally went to sleep, however, it had passed over, and there was only the sound of rain falling upon the deck.

XVII

*B*ELLA had made up her mind that Roger must return the money he had won from Mr. Ransom on the last hand. But when the bugle woke her on the following morning, to bright sunlight and a fresh cool wind, the ladies' cabin was empty.

"Viney," she called.

The washroom door opened, and Viney came through with a broad smile.

"Morning, Mis' Willcox."

"Good morning, Viney. When did Mrs. Ransom get up?"

"Oh, she's done dressed and et her breakfas' and lef' the boat."

"Left the boat?"

"Yes, mis'. Her and Mr. Ransom done got off at Sy'cuse. She said fo' me not to wake you, mis'."

"Thank you, Viney. I'll get up now."

"Yes, mis'."

As Bella dressed leisurely, she saw that there was nothing she could do. She knew only their name. She had no idea where they lived. But she thought she would always remember Mrs. Ransom as the loveliest person she had ever met.

The saloon seemed strangely empty. Only one place was laid at table—the others had finished and gone on deck. Bella could hear their feet walking back and forth above her head.

She smiled mechanically at the steward as he brought her peach and took her order for eggs and tea and toast. He was a young man with a long Hibernian lip, a sober mouth, and dancing gray eyes.

"It's a fine morning, this morning, ma'am."

"Isn't it?" said Bella.

He disappeared into his kitchen, to return finally with Bella's eggs, golden and white; he set down her tea with a flourish and some slop, begged her pardon, and mopped untidily with a wet rag.

"Wasn't the thunder terrible, though?" he asked.

"It was quite a storm," Bella said, looking up at his long face.

He nodded. "My knees rattled like beads, ma'am. And the gentlemen calling for whiskey most of the night, too, and me giving my soul for a drink of the same, but the captain was up, ma'am, watching the play." He slapped at a fly with his rag and leaned heavily on the table. "The gentry had some heavy play—indeed yes. Oh, you should have seen it, ma'am. And Mr. Willcox as steady as a hog on ice. 'Give me two cards,' he says. And he looks at 'em, and puts up ten dollars like the President of the United States."

"What time shall we get to Buffalo?" Bella asked.

"Sometime tomorrow morning, ma'am. The captain's half killing the horses. Three fines since sunrise for speeding, with the wash on the banks like the ocean waves. 'Give it to the commission,' he says, howlding out ten dollars. 'Haven't they anny ambition,' he says, 'damn their souls?' Begging your pardon, ma'am."

"Three hours ahead of time? That's wonderful, isn't it?"

"Yes, ma'am. 'Lather the lazy beast,' says the captain. 'If he falls down dead I'll put the collar round me own neck,' he says. He says if we can pick up two hours between here and Buffalo we'll have the record, ma'am. I've got ten shilling on it with the steersman."

Bella smiled at his excited face.

"I hope you'll win, then."

The steward grinned and thanked her and retreated with abrupt bashfulness to his kitchen.

Through the open door to the steersman's deck, Bella saw Roger's legs. The cry, "Bridge! Low bridge!" came and echoed.

Bella's heart flopped when she saw his face. His eyes would not meet hers. They wore circles, and were tired and bewildered. As they were alone together, she lifted her mouth for a kiss, but his lips missed hers and barely brushed her cheek. He sat down across the table from her and asked how she had slept.

"Not very well till after the storm."

He stared moodily out of the window.

"It must have been hot in there, especially for you with a headache. I wish I hadn't got into that card game."

She said, "It was better for me to get to bed, Roger."

He put his hands on the table and stared at them.

"What did you think of Mr. Atterbury?" he asked suddenly.

"Mr. Atterbury? Why, I liked him very much."

She spoke brightly, trying to catch his eye and give him a smile. He looked so upset, she wanted to comfort him. If he wanted to play cards, she didn't care, as long as he loved her. But she did not know how to go about it without hurting his feelings.

Roger nodded.

"I liked him very much myself. Mr. Ransom said he thought he was a very gentlemanly sort."

He seemed to derive a meager comfort from that. Then he looked up at Bella, meeting her smile.

"Bella—"

"Yes, Roger."

She put her teacup down carefully.

But he was silent, moodily examining his hands again.

She tried to divert his thoughts. "It won't be long," she said softly, reaching out to cover his

restless hands with her own. "The steward says
we shall get into Buffalo tomorrow morning.
We'll take a stage for Niagara the first thing and
go right down to the hotel."

But he didn't respond. He said, "Bella—oh,
Lord!" and swallowed. He looked so miserable

that she thought she had better tell him that she knew.

"I understand, Roger dear. I was awake last night. Mrs. Ransom and I went out on the front deck and we were out there when Mr. Atterbury went off the boat with Mr. Jason. We heard them talking. So don't bother to tell me. I don't mind, as long as we're together. What if he did win most of our money? He said you'd won the last hand and that will leave us enough."

Roger looked at her for a long time.

"You don't understand," he said. "When we found Atterbury had jumped the boat, all of us understood that he must be a professional gambler and that the game had been crooked. And we looked at the cards this morning and found that on the last hand he had better cards than mine. He used them only to run up Mr. Ransom's betting. Then he dropped out. I don't know why. The cards were marked."

For a moment Bella felt a prick of friendliness for Mr. Atterbury.

"Perhaps he wasn't all bad," she said.

"No. Perhaps not. But, Bella, when I found that out I couldn't keep Ransom's money. You see, he'd told me he and his wife were planning to take a sort of second honeymoon together. They couldn't very well after last night. He didn't want to take it back, but I made him."

He let out his breath.

"I don't mind losing money to a gambler. But I couldn't take what should have been Ransom's. Do you mind very much?"

He looked at her squarely, but she could see the question in his mind. Then she saw his eyes change and she could read some of the change, too. She had taken away her hand and was sitting very straight in her chair. She felt unexplainably happy and proud.

"Mind? Roger, do you want to know something?"

"Yes." A hint of the old teasing look came round his eyes.

"I'm the happiest woman on earth this morning. Do you know why?"

"No," he said soberly.

"Because I'm your wife."

She looked so gallant and so eager and so small. He thought she had the same look in her eyes that she had when she watched the hawk, and he had made fun of her. And Bella, watching him, felt that a barrier between them had just been broken down. He knew it too, she thought; it seemed to her that in its breaking down they had just become aware of its existence.

He said suddenly, "Don't just sit there looking beautiful. Come here."

But when she came round the table to join him he swung her up off her feet, and kissed her, practically in mid-air.

XVIII

*T*HEY went on deck together. The steersman greeted them cheerfully. The team were trotting with pricked ears. The wind was fresh and clear to breathe. Mr. and Mrs. Neilson had chairs in the lee of the saloon on the steersman's deck. Mr. L. D. Jones was sitting on the saloon deck, his legs stretched out in front of him, his back to the wind, puffing his segar. For a wonder it was burning, and the smoke came out as thick as the smoke from the galley pipe.

The captain waved to them from the bow deck and shouted, "Morning!"

"Let's go down to him," Roger said.

They edged forward along the outside cat-walk, Roger steadying his wife, though she needed no help, while her skirts whipped back to entangle his knees. The captain was smoking a deep cob pipe. He pointed the stem at the team.

"Brand-new," he said. "They're pulling me faster than any I've ever been hitched to."

"They look fine and fat, don't they?" said Bella.

"They do," said the captain. "Poor devils, they don't know any better."

Bella and Roger sat down and let the wind

blow over them, while the captain walked up and down, three steps each way. Now and then he pulled out his watch.

"Young man," he said suddenly, "I'm going to get you to Buffalo the fastest any honeymoon pair got there in the history of the United States."

Roger and Bella laughed and he laughed back, boomingly, one hand steadying his beard.

"Who's that coming?" Bella pointed to an old man walking the towpath, with a bag full of straw on one shoulder and a long stick in the opposite hand.

"Bank watch," said the captain, and shouted, "Hello, Hank!"

"Hey!" cried the old man. "You're traveling." He touched the towline with his stick, letting it slide along till the angle carried it out of reach. "You're busting the limit."

"Wide open and ready to fry!" yelled the captain. "Watch the wash. They've had the hurry-up boats tailing us from Schenectady."

"What is a hurry-up boat?" Bella asked.

The captain bowed courteously to her. It was obvious that he enjoyed being asked questions by a pretty girl.

"It's the gang that mends the big leaks. The bank watch can stuff ratholes with the straw he carries. But a big leak needs a gang with shovels. And when they're wanted, they're wanted in a hurry, Mrs. Willcox."

The team slowed a little on the drag of a sharp bend, and the steersman had to go neat to avoid a line boat coming towards them. It was close, and the captain addressed some general remarks towards the line-boat steersman. Then he turned back to his passengers with a wave of his hand.

"You going straight to Niagara?"

"I don't know," Roger said. "I've not got much money left."

The captain looked sober.

"I didn't know that cuss, though I didn't fancy his looks. I'll know him next time. We've no law against cards, but I won't have sharpers on my boat. Did he skin you clean?"

"Very nearly," Roger admitted wryly. "I've got only ten dollars left for our week there, and no hotel would put us up for that."

"It's a damn shame." The captain pursed his

lips. "I'll tell you, though. If you wouldn't mind boarding on a farm, I'm pretty sure I know of one. My sister married a farmer," he said rather diffidently. "They live pretty close to the falls, about two miles down the Lewiston road. They've got a nice house and my sister's clean and there's only one child. They had bad luck with their crops last season and they'd be glad of boarders."

Bella and Roger exchanged glances.

"I could catch the mail out of Rochester," said the captain, "and send them a letter to say you're coming. They'd get it tomorrow, because the driver drops their post for them."

He turned tactfully to curse the driver boy for letting the horses loaf. Under cover of his exhortations, Roger said, "What do you think?"

"Let's," said Bella.

When they told the captain, he beamed on them.

"I'll go right down and commence the letter now. I ought to have it ready when we reach Rochester," he said.

They stayed out all day, watching the small new towns slide by, seeing the boats coming east with their smell of wheat and new flour, or livestock; overtaking west-bound boats, with ploughs on board, machinery, ironware, and merchandise or immigrants with round staring eyes. All along the canal the harvest was going forward. They saw men cradling oats and barley, fields of buckwheat beginning to turn; they saw the stage overtake them, pursued by its own dust. They saw the treetops at Irondequoit far under them as they crossed on the embankment; and they saw the sun setting as they came into Rochester.

The captain dispatched Viney on a frantic race to the Eagle Tavern with his completed letter, and as the packet hauled out of town they left supper and went on deck once more, to see the town wane behind them, with its numberless bridges, clacking mills, and thundering falls. The long arms of sunset shrank. Darkness came as they wound through the small farms, the towpath hemmed with fences. Then they floated into the woods again, skirting the Tonawanda swamp, where sycamores lifted ghostly arms to the starlight and thousands of blackbirds started up at their passage.

XIX

*I*T WAS only after they had turned into the road to Lewiston that Bella realized she was a prisoner in Fate's hands. The arrival at Buffalo had found her prepared and excited. They had docked soon after breakfast.

The captain was interviewed on deck by a writing representative of the *Advertiser*, who came down into the saloon and asked for Mrs. and Mr. Willcox's impression of the trip. "They spoke enthusiastically of the service," he wrote down, "and Mrs. Willcox observed that the speed was exhilarating." While the captain continued to receive congratulations under the proud chaperonage of the company agent, she and Roger walked down the basin to the lake shore and out along the mole.

The lake was vivid blue that morning; there were small somnolent clouds high up, and cat's-paw ripples on the water; gulls wheeled, monotonously calling, perpetually unhurried, awkward birds made graceful by the sky. Way to the west, sky and lake merged in a drift of haze. And, looking at a schooner slowly growing out of the perspective, Bella was aware of the largeness of the earth, and for the first time in her life she lost all sense of her own smallness of stature. As she stood hand in hand with her husband, she could feel the forces in her taking form and gaining strength.

"It must be like the sea, Roger."

She had never seen the sea. She was destined never to see it; but she did not know that.

His only reply was the pressure of his hand. Thinking how handsome he looked, she would have liked to ask what he was thinking of; but intuition closed her lips.

They lingered till the schooner had docked and watched as the dock hands invested her, and the gulls that had followed her in wheeled intricately over the dock, dropping discordant cries.

Then the captain came to them and said he had found a carriage and driver who would take them to his brother-in-law's farm for a matter of a dollar and a half. The man wanted to start at once.

They hurriedly returned to the *Western Lion* to get their bags. The carriage, a dearborn with an extra seat and no top, was waiting for them, the driver sitting with his legs crossed. He only nodded when they said good morning.

Viney and the steward had brought up their bags and a lunch the captain had ordered for them. The whole packet crew wished them luck. But the driver cut short their farewells, whipping up his horses and putting them to a tremendous burst. Once they were out of sight of the canal, however, he slowed down to a jogtrot and kept to it.

Bella did not mind how slowly they went. Her nerves were exquisitely keyed. She noticed every flower, every wayside nest. And she found Roger glad to share them with her.

The driver granted them half an hour's stop for lunch, and they took it away from the road to a piece of meadow under the supervision of a couple of dull-eyed ewes. They lay on their backs in the sun, so that Bella felt the grass through her dress, even the crossing of blades, and she smelled the small scents that one finds only close to earth, and she wondered whether her Christian upbringing had abandoned her, but she did not care.

The driver climbed back into the wagon when he judged that the proper time had arrived for continuing the journey, and Roger came to life again and helped her pack the remains of their luncheon. Their hands became shy at the work of gathering papers and they did not look at each other. When they were in the wagon once more, Bella became conscious of a strange breathlessness upon the earth. She felt it in herself. As if they also felt it, cows and horses at pasture lifted their heads to watch her pass, and when she was by and looked back at them she found them still inscrutably staring after the wagon.

It was only when the driver turned them into the road for Lewiston that she realized at last there was no turning back. She had come too far. All that she had been accustomed to lay four days behind her, three and a half by the record run of a packet boat. She had put herself into life's hands, and now she must go on with it.

She longed to take Roger's hand and beg him to be good to her, never to hurt her, never to deceive her. But when her hand touched his and he looked at her, her face tilted with its old cock of the chin, and she smiled.

"Darling."

Roger sounded choky. His hand hurt hers, and for an instant she wanted to cry to the driver to turn back. But in the same impulse her hand resigned itself to the hurt and returned it. She was alive. She was alive in every nerve, and her heart raced.

She saw the Franklins' house ahead of them, a low white house set behind trees, with a red barn at an angle. A middle-aged woman was staring toward them from the gate. Her eyes were curious, but kindly. She smiled as they turned into the yard, and came over to stand by the wheel.

"I'm real pleased to meet you, Mr. and Mrs. Willcox. We'll try to make you comfortable, me and my husband."

She took their bags in her strong hands and

111

led them into the house. She showed them the parlor with windows freshly opened, but still with a faint musty taste in the air.

"This-here's to be your setting room for your own. Me and Jim won't come into it while you're here."

She paused, and Bella collected her wits.

"It's a lovely room, isn't it, Roger?"

"Yes, it is."

Roger looked embarrassed. His eyes swung wildly about the walls as if seeking an object on which to comment, and Bella was amused at the proud smile Mrs. Franklin bestowed on him. Coughing discreetly, the woman led them upstairs to a bedroom three quarters filled by an old double bed that was piled deep in feather ticks.

"Oh, it *is* lovely," Bella said.

The ceiling followed the slope of the roof, and the window was a broad dormer that looked directly into the branches of a maple tree.

"I'm glad you like it, Mrs. Willcox," said Mrs. Franklin, adding practically, "The bed is a real good one, too. Real comfortable. Them are goose-feather ticks."

She edged her way to the door.

"Now I've showed you over. I always think it's easiest for persons to learn their way about first off. My husband can show Mr. Willcox anything else. Supper is any time to suit you after milking.

I'll bring it to you in the parlor." She smiled and slipped away.

They sat by the open window for a long time, witnessing the order of the evening unfolding itself in the pattern of the farm. First came Mr. Franklin home behind his team, walking beside the load of barley, pitchfork on shoulder, while a small boy shrilly drove. The small boy slid down the load at the barn door and whistled to a shepherd dog; his father drove the team into the mow and left the wagon there, and the team strode with loose strides and jingling traces for the stable. In a little while he came to the kitchen for a glass of buttermilk. He was a middle-aged man, with thick curved shoulders and a smooth-shaven, reddened face. Then the boy brought in the cows, the dog officious at their heels, and Mrs. Franklin carried the pails across the yard to help with the milking. It was so still in the yard that Bella imagined she could hear the spurt of milk against the pail. The sun was sinking through the tree branches, and a robin hopped along a bough and began to call. A veery in the woods beyond the pasture bars made answer.

"Let's unpack, Roger, so the room will seem our own."

They hung their clothes side by side from wooden pegs under a curtained shelf, lingering in the work to look at them and then at each other. When they had finished, Roger kissed her almost shyly.

"It seems as if we'd lived here, doesn't it?"

His voice expressed his masculine amazement at a settled room.

Bella only nodded and led the way downstairs. There they were introduced to Mr. Franklin, who made them welcome simply and then supplied Roger with the final geographical details of the household. Bella asked for the little boy, but his mother said that he had gone off on an errand. While they were having their supper in the parlor, they heard him come in and sneak upstairs. Coming down again, he gave them an awed welcome over the rail.

They waited till they heard the farmer and his wife retiring in the room behind the parlor. Then they went up together. At the door of their room they understood the little boy's errand. A large bunch of white clover and daisies stood on the washstand, filling the room with scent. The candle quavered in Bella's hand.

"Wasn't it sweet of them, Roger?"

For answer he stooped and blew out the candle.

Bella's breath caught. She set the candlestick down in the dark. She let her hands fall, then turned slowly and faced him.

XX

*T*HEY liked the farm. They liked the Franklins. The little boy could not overcome his puzzlement at the thought of two strangers staying in his parents' house. But even he, after two days, came to accept them guardedly.

They took their lunch next morning and wandered off across the fields. They found a narrow path in the woods and went down it till they came to the edge of a stream, and followed this up to a broad still pool whose sides seemed mortared by the roots of trees. It was far back from anywhere and it was not deep, but it was deep enough for Roger to cool himself in. As Bella lay back on the bank, idly watching him wallow in the deeper portions, she wondered at the delight she found in what she had been taught to hold indecent. But the sight of Roger, or of her own slimness, or the quiet of the woods gave her heart whatever answer she needed.

They were silent often, but when they spoke, what they said mattered deeply to them both. And in the late afternoon they returned, Roger fishing the likely holes with worms selected for him by the little boy.

Mrs. Franklin fed them suppers of simple homely food in the parlor, and afterwards they sat out a conventional half hour in the kitchen and talked to the woman and her husband. Then hand in hand they went up the narrow stairs to their room, undressing in the dark.

It was on the sixth morning of their stay that Bella said, "We ought to go over to Niagara Falls, I suppose."

"I suppose so," Roger said.

They looked at each other gloomily, then suddenly burst out laughing.

"Why in heaven's name ought we to do anything?"

Bella looked at him demurely.

"I ought to write Mamma. I believe five days is the proper lapse for a lady in my case, and here it is going on ten."

"Is it?"

Bella said, "We could walk over and take our lunch."

"I suppose we could. But there was a trout in that third pool."

"There's tomorrow."

"But today looks right."

"I don't really want to go," said Bella.

But they consulted Mr. Franklin, who did not

116

see why they should walk. He said it would be much simpler if he drove them over that very morning, and if they did not care about looking at the falls too long he could get them back by noon. He would be glad to spare the time for them.

So they were driven over, and viewed the falls, and came back in time to take their lunch to the pool. But Bella left Roger on his belly seeking his trout and returned dutifully to write her letter.

She wrote it at the washstand beside the window, with the clover close to her nose. She found it hard to write, partly because she always found writing a task, partly because she knew that what mattered for her to say would not find favor in her mother's reading, and partly because of something in the room that troubled her.

She looked up several times from her paper to see what it might be, but she could not put her finger on it. And finally she folded the letter and opened it again to read what she had written.

DEAR MAMMA—

I am writing here to tell you that I am very happy, and that I do believe that Roger is the most delightful man I ever met. We are both very well, and send our wishes that you may be also. The weather was most delightful all the way, except for one short storm, but it was not very severe. And since we have been here it has been lovely all the time.

117

We were both very much awed by the falls. They are much grander than the human mind can possibly conceive until it has encountered them. While we examined them, I could not prevent a wish that Lord Byron might have viewed them that their magnificence might be preserved in verse.

Your devoted daughter,

BELLA W.

P. S. Please tell Papa that we made the packet voyage in less than four days. They told us it was the fastest ever made.

She approved thoroughly of the sentence about Lord Byron, knowing that it would gratify her mother, but she giggled as she read it.

Casting an eye over the note, she dipped her pen to add:—

Please give Clorinda and Papa my best love.

She stopped, feeling the beat of her heart. Her best love—that was for her family. Her eyes turned to the bed, where she had tossed down Roger's coat. She understood now as she stared at the empty sleeves. She was in love, with Roger— plain love.

Her breast rose and her eyes filled as she stared round the little room. Her mind was pervaded by a tragic sense that she would remember it as long as she lived, so that, if she were magically transplanted in her sleep, even though she might be an old woman she would rise up without the candle and move unerringly. And she knew that her first

118

action would be to feel for the empty coat and take it up, as she did now.

She stood with it at the window, watching her young husband marching home across the pasture, hot, disheveled, triumphantly bearing his trout on a forked stick.

END